Noise That Stays Noise

Cole Swensen

Noise That Stays Noise

ESSAYS

THE UNIVERSITY OF MICHIGAN PRESS

Ann Arbor

Published in the United States of America by
The University of Michigan Press
Printed and bound by CPI Group (UK) Ltd, Croydon, CR0 4YY

2014   2013   2012   2011   4   3   2   1

A CIP catalog record for this book is available from the British Library.

Library of Congress Cataloging-in-Publication Data

Swensen, Cole
    Noise that stays noise : essays / Cole Swensen.
        p.   cm. — (Poets on poetry)
    ISBN 978-0-472-07155-5 (cloth : acid-free paper) —
    ISBN 978-0-472-05155-7 (pbk. : acid-free paper) —
    ISBN 978-0-472-02771-2 (e-book)
        1. Poetry.   2. Poetics.   I. Title.

    PS3569.W384N64   2011
    814'.54—dc22   2011011896

To my mother, Patricia Swensen, and my husband, Anthony Hayward

Preface

In his *ABC of Reading*, Ezra Pound defined literature as "news that stays news," evoking the immediacy that literature can attain and retain, the way that it can capture life almost before it's conditioned by language—almost, but not quite, for while the language of news may be uncommonly fresh, it's still entirely shaped by convention. Much experimentation in twentieth- and twenty-first-century poetry has tried to get beyond that convention by finding ways to keep language molten, to keep it in motion, a possibility itself based on the belief that there's something that precedes news, that there exists a state of language more raw, more volatile, with its own unique potentials not only for presenting experience, but also for expanding it.

The following essays explore various writers and ideas engaged with such a state of language, often using paradigms from other disciplines for the additional perspectives that they offer. In particular, the paradigm of self-organization from noise, borrowed from the biological and information sciences, presides over the collection as a whole, for it suggests a way that language-arts practices that are initially impenetrable to a given reader can become recognized by that reader as powerful in their own right while also enlarging the field of the sayable, and thus of the thinkable, the imaginable, for the culture as a whole.

The geometry inherent in literary structures is also an interest that directs much of this collection—as are the relationships of the visual to the verbal and the source text to the translated text. All can be seen as part of a larger question regarding the shape of experience, and I have tried through the ordering of these pieces to make their inter-relationships apparent. What emerges, perhaps above all, is the primary place of relationship itself, and of the particular shape of relationship as dimensionless articulation, as the principle of articulation in both its meanings, and in a way that fuses them.

A note about the figures and illustrations that accompany some of these pieces: after much discussion about cost and reproducibility, we (author, series editor, press editor, and production team) decided that the best way to get these images to readers in a quality high enough to be intriguing and/or to make the point they're supposed to make would be, in fact, to send readers to the Internet, supplying them (you) with the specific search words that will get you to high-quality versions of these images quickly. On the one hand, I'm sorry about this because I like to think that reading can and does happen anywhere and everywhere, and in particular, that it is not becoming dependent upon the computer. Much would be lost by that; I think we all value reading as its own machine-free technology—versatile, flexible, and amazingly portable.

On the other hand, the Internet can deliver you much better quality images, and more of them, than we could in print. For instance, the Adolf Wolfli images alluded to in the "A Hand Writing" essay: we could have reproduced one, maybe two, of these stunning pieces, and most likely only in black and white; whereas through the Internet, you'll be able not only to see dozens of full-color images, but also to access all sorts of other information on Wolfi's life and work. To return to Pound: it was he who, in his *Cantos,* gave us the Modernist model of the exploding book—the book that doesn't want to keep its readers neatly tucked within, but that wants instead to send them out into the world to explore all the people, events, ideas, etc., that he brings into the work. In making our choice to use the Internet in this way, we had him and his tradition in mind.

This choice also gives this book the chance to enact the overflow, the enabling excess, that it so frequently mentions and that forms another organizing principle of these pieces. It is the inability to be contained—within a given genre, a given technology, a given language, or even a given definition of language—that has allowed contemporary poetry to rethink language into a method of enlarging the sayable, and thus enlarging the world.

Acknowledgments

I would like to thank the following editors and publishers who first published some of these essays in journals and collections: *American Letters & Commentary* 13, Summer 2001, edited by Anna Rabinowitz ("To Writewithize"); *American Poetry in the Twenty-First Century*, edited by Claudia Rankine and Lisa Sewell, Wesleyan University Press, 2008 ("Peter Gizzi's City"); *Conjunctions*, edited by Brad Morrow ("For M. Moore," "Besides, of Bedouins," and "And And"); *Drunken Boat #9*, 2008, edited by Ravi Shankar and Jean-Jacques Poucel ("In Praise of Error"); *Faire Part*, winter issue, 2009 ("The Infinite Mountain" in French translation); *je te continue ma lecture*, P.O.L, 1999 ("Quand le corps est une phrase à venir," translated into French by Juliette Valéry); *Moving Borders: Three Decades of Innovative Writing by Women*, edited by Mary Margaret Sloan, Talisman Books, 1998 ("Against the Limits of Language"); *Multiformalisms: Postmodern Poetics of Form*, edited by Annie Finch and Susan Schultz, Texto Books, Cincinnati, Ohio, 2009 ("Seeing Reading: Susan Howe's Moving Margins"); *Poetry Foundation Website*, edited by Emily Warn and Nick Twemlow ("Cy Twombly: *Hero & Leandro*"); *Theorie, Littérature, Epsitémologie* #25, Presse Universitaires de Vincenne, 2008 ("Translating Timbre," translated into French by Noëlle Batt and Yves Arbrioux).

I would also like to thank the following conferences, events, and institutions for which some of these pieces were written:

AFEA conference at the Bibliothèque nationale, Paris, 2007

Associated Writers and Writing Programs annual conferences, 2008 and 2009

Attention/Inattention Conference, University of Denver, 2005

Contemporary Translation conference at the University
of Georgia, Athens, 2008
Ecole normale superior in Lyon
EEL conference, Denver, 2004
PEN World Voices Conference, New York, May 2009
Pulitzer Museum, St. Louis
Temple University
Translated Acts Conference at Central St. Martins, Lon-
don, 2008
University of Arizona Poetry Center

And I would like to thank Simone Fattal of Post Apollo Press and
Stephen Ratcliffe for permission to reprint Stephen Ratcliffe's
poems, and Devin Johnston of Flood Editions and John Taggart
for permission to reprint John Taggart's poems, in the essay on
their works. I would also like to thank André Dimanche, Editeur,
Awede Press, Coffee House Press, Farrar, Straus, and Giroux,
Gallimard, Graywolf Press, New Directions Press, Omnidawn
Press, P.O.L, University of California Press, Wesleyan Press, and
Sun & Moon Press for their making available so much vital contemporary poetry from which I have taken excerpts in accor-
dance with the doctrine of fair use.

Contents

Noise That Stays Noise: Generative Abymes

Noise That Stays Noise   3

Bones: Mallarmé's Dice Game   12

Olson and the Projective   16

Against the Limits of Language: Geometry in the Work of Anne-Marie Albiach and Susan Howe   21

Seeing Reading: Susan Howe's Moving Margins   32

The Infinite Mountain: Nicolas Pesquès   41

Peter Gizzi's City: The Political Quotidian   45

News That Stays News   53

News That Stays News: Generative Bridges

To Writewithize   69

How Ekphrasis Makes Art   74

A Hand Writing   82

The Fold   90

Translating Writing/Writing Translation   96

In Praise of Error   100

Translating Timbre   106

Translating the Visible: The Incommensurability of Image   113

The Ghost of Translation   119

Homages

For M. Moore 125

Besides, of Bedouins—On *Hotel Lautréamont* by
John Ashbery 131

Cy Twombly, *Hero & Leandro* 1981–84 140

Andscape: The Serial Paintings of Etel Adnan 144

And And 148

Quand le corps est une phrase à venir:
Claude Royet-Journoud 151

Noise That Stays Noise

GENERATIVE ABYMES

Noise That Stays Noise

It really comes back to posing the question: *How to
speak of that for which we do not yet have an adequate
language?*

—Henri Atlan

Noise—a subjective category if there ever was one—is something
most of us try to avoid, but in the stricter definition of information science, it's an essential, perhaps even distinguishing, element of an artistic text. The experience of confusion or of
nonunderstanding that for many people frequently accompanies the first reading of a poem is often a product of such noise
working in concert with the information also contained in the
text. The degree of nonunderstanding in a given piece changes
from reader to reader and is often slight; the novel feeling it
occasions is part of the pleasure of reading poetry and is the
source of the simultaneous suspension and surprise that seems
to bypass the cognitive faculties. In mild cases, the reader doesn't
notice the noise as such; however, at other times it is sufficient to
impede the reader's full appreciation, at which point he or she
often chooses to reread the piece, often many more times. During those rereadings, some of the noise is organized into information—perhaps factual, emotional, or formal—that augments
the initial appreciation of the piece. This process, which, bor-
rowing a term from the biological sciences, I'm going to refer to
as self-organization from noise, is particularly important in considering much recent American poetry, which often contains a
lot of what many would consider noise.

Yuri Lotman described textual noise as the "remainder after
complete translation," which interestingly recalls Frost's comment that "poetry is what's left after translation" and points to
poeticity itself, in other words, the nonsemantic linguistic effects,

as constituting noise. The statement also underscores the notion of a "remainder" as an important element of poetry. Such an approach demands that we consider a literary text solely as an act of communication, as a completely quantifiable message passing through a channel from a sender to a receiver. Though this may strike some as cold, on the contrary, I think it is just such an approach that can elucidate the ways in which literature differs from mechanistic models of communication and can, unlike them, augment the quantifiable with irreducible qualities of human sensation and emotion.

The concept of "noise" in this sense can be traced back to the Macy conferences on cybernetics, which were held in New York in the late 1940s and early '50s. These ideas were further developed and used in communication studies by Heinz Von Foerster at the University of Illinois in the early '60s. Since then, they have been increasingly applied to the theory of information, which was developed by Claude Shannon in the 1940s. In his work, Shannon chose to look at information not qualitatively, but quantitatively; from this perspective he developed the probabilistic equations that form the basis of mathematical information theory. The main goal of that theory has little in common with literature: it is simply to reduce the number of signals needed to transmit a given quantity of information and to insure its minimal alteration in transmission.

Information theory has numerous commercial applications, from improving phone lines to increasing the accuracy of electronic exchanges, and is concerned not with the meaning of messages, but with their construction and transmission. Someone working on such projects or applications is always working against noise. Noise is most simply defined as any signal, interruption, or disturbance in the channel of communication that alters the quantity or quality of transmitted information. It does not necessarily have anything to do with sound; it is called noise because the phenomenon first surfaced in relation to radio transmissions, in which audible disturbances such as static posed the greatest problems. However, in a text, various idiosyncrasies from typographical errors to intentional ambiguities can also be considered noise if they too alter (or augment) the imparted information.

Information, in turn, can be defined in terms of the resolution of uncertainty. Taking the simplest possible case, if a receiver is waiting for a yes or no answer to a posed question, the receipt of one piece of information out of the possible two—for instance, yes—completely resolves the receiver's uncertainty. If, however the response the receiver is waiting for is one of the twenty-six letters of our alphabet, his or her uncertainty is much greater, so the response, Q, for instance, resolves more uncertainty and so is said to convey more information. In most actual cases of transmission, the various possibilities are not equally probable; therefore, information is defined as the probability that a particular element out of the many possible will arrive.

Claude Shannon's mathematical formulas have important similarities with the formulas that define entropy, which describes the probability of particular arrangements of molecules in a given system. These similarities allowed Shannon to posit a basic relationship between the two: a system low in entropy equates to one high in information. Entropy correlates with the degree of organization in a system, and its process is described by the second law of thermodynamics, which states that in any closed system, disorder will only increase. As high information is characterized by high organization, there is an inverse relationship between information and entropy.

The theory of information, however, must also take into account redundancy; for instance, the sequence "AAAAAAAA" is highly organized but not very informative because it is also highly redundant; in contrast, the sequence ALPHABET is again highly organized but also informative because each element is novel in its combination of character and placement.[1] Both novelty and redundancy have a place in our interpretation of the world around us. Complete novelty would give us a world like that of Oliver Sacks's "man without a memory,"[2] for whom the world was incomprehensible and frightening; complete redundancy, on the other hand, would amount to the heat death of complete homogeneity.

An ideal communication is one in which entropy is 0 and all information imparted is received unaltered. This, however, is almost never the case; a message is usually degraded or altered, at least to a small degree, in its transmission, and these alterations prevent the receiver's uncertainty from being completely resolved—and may have even added some new uncertainties. To go back to the example above, suppose you were waiting for a message composed of a single word, and it arrived as АЛЛНАВДТ. Your original uncertainty would be for the most part resolved, but the suppression of two characters (or rather, their replacement by others that at the moment don't appear meaningful because they don't seem to share a system with the others) would keep you from feeling completely certain. In this instance, the alterations at those two points would be noise because they reduce the certainty of the information you received. If you have other sources of the same information, you might very well receive similar, but not identical, information from them. The similarities supply a necessary redundancy, stabilizing the message (which is to say that the appropriate characters will be reinforced and the missing ones may well be supplied), while the differences supply noise. This noise may be entirely useless; however, suppose those other sources of the same information each also included Cyrillic characters, but different ones in different places. Those individual bits of noise might, taken together, form a word that has meaning in a different context, in this case in Russian. In such a case, you will have received the intended message, plus an additional one if you can organize what was initially noise into a meaningful Russian word.

Though the above example greatly oversimplifies information theory, I have used it because it deals with human messages in a code of language, rather than messages being sent and received by technical apparatuses in digital codes, which is the type of system that information theory usually deals with. Within the latter sort of system, noise is always an impediment; in literature, however, noise is not necessarily something to be suppressed, as it constitutes the potential for increasing the complexity of the system of which it is a part.

One of the reasons literature can use noise constructively is that any literary work is composed not just of one sender-channel-receiver system, but of many. In this way, a literary work has more in common with a biological organism than it does with an electronic transmission, and several theorists have proposed that the work currently being done on self-organization from noise in theoretical biology might have applications to literary studies. Researchers in physics, sociology, and political science have also made use of the paradigm of self-organization from noise to enrich their perspectives.[3]

One of the biologists best known for his work on this paradigm is Henri Atlan, author of numerous books, including *Entre le cristal et la fumée*.[4] In this book, Atlan examines the way noise in a given system is incorporated into more complex, and useful, information by the system immediately above the original system in an hierarchically arranged biological organism. The idea connects with literary studies on two levels. One is by assuming that a literary work is in some ways analogous to a biological organism, as noted above. The other, a more direct application, considers the way the reader, who is of course literally a biological organism and an integral part of the complex communication system that is literature, processes the combination of information and noise that he or she encounters when reading.

Noise in a complex system (a system itself composed of many subsystems) has a different character from that of noise in a radio transmission. Jean-Claude Tabary, a French neuro-biologist who studies the effects of noise on the nervous systems of various organisms, defines noise in such a complex system as the difference between the effects of a stimulus and the possibilities of the organism's immediately assimilating that stimulus. The process of self-organization from noise, he goes on to say, is based on the capacity of that organism to reduce that difference.[5] This definition underscores the relative and subjective nature of noise in this context.

Literary noise must be defined differently, though, because it is often not a degradation of the message; on the contrary, such noise is often intentional and aimed at preventing the suppression of imagination that complete certainty can cause. So for poetry, a more useful definition of noise might take Lotman's and add to it the difference between the degree of decipherability that the reader expects and what she or he actually encounters on the page. This would include poeticity—the unquantifiable qualities of sound relationships, word associations, and innate rhythms—but also things that intentionally disrupt the smooth flow of information, such as fragmentation, unusual syntax, ambiguity, neologism, juxtaposition, alternative logics, graphic spacing, etc.—in other words, any alteration to the basic linguistic code. And different from its appearance in biological and information science, the noise in literary works is often not arbitrary or unpredictable; in fact, it is usually more predictable than not. Its limits of possibility are determined by the piece of which it's a part, and thus a given piece can condition us to its noise by degrees. As a given instance of noise in a text is often part of a pattern of similar constructions, it conditions us also through redundancy, creating a stable base for its differences.

Each source of noise corresponds to a different subsystem of the poem, such as the denotative system, the metaphoric system, the image system, the syntactical system, the rhythmic system, the system of sound relationships, and so on. What is information to any one of these subsystems may be noise to the others; for instance, the syntactical system may create difficulties for an appreciation of the denotative system in isolation (odd syntax can make it more difficult for a reader to know literally what is being said). Both systems are in themselves instances of organization, and these organizations can interfere with each other. However, at a "higher" level of organization, such as that of the entire poem, they can work together to create a more complex body of information. The more we look at possible sources and manifestations of noise, the more it seems that in terms of all literature, but most acutely with poetry, information itself must be redefined. It can't be limited to Claude Shannon's quantifiable. Perhaps poetry itself can be defined as those literary instances of language in which the nonquantifiable aspects of its information overshadow the quantifiable.

In this light, Michel Serres offers a particularly useful perspective. He bases his definition of noise on its etymology; the word shares a common root with "nautical" and "navy," associations that reveal its original relationship to the sea,[6] and thus connect noise with ideas of endless motion and unorganized energy, with the "white noise" that is the background sound of the sea and which for Serres is the basis of being. It is the background against which any information figures and out of which any information emerges. So rather than constituting an extra element that invades information, here noise is the default state of all information, that out of which information organizes itself or is organized. "Noise is not a phenomenon; all phenomena separate from it. . . . As soon as there is a phenomenon, it leaves noise, as soon as an appearance arises, it does so by masking the noise. Thus it is not phenomenology but being itself."[7] The way in which poets define noise strongly influences style, with those holding closer to Lotman's definition falling, along today's aesthetic spectrum, toward the conservative end. At the other end of that spectrum would be those sharing Serres's definition.

Readers of poetry also fall along a similar spectrum, some finding noise beyond Lotman's "that which cannot be translated" difficult to assimilate; others may be able to work greater degrees of noise comfortably into the possibilities that they're already entertaining, effectively defusing it, while yet another type of reader may accept the noise, but not fully assimilate it, thus letting it retain some of its disquieting indeterminacy as it also augments the piece. This last sort of reader will be reading a richer, more complex poem, a poem composed of more than words, for, unlike other language uses and even other forms of literature, poetry is the one place where noise is not only organized into information, but has value *in remaining noise*. The unassimilable has value because in a literary context, "to assimilate" means "to translate into another code," yet poetry can endlessly incorporate, constitute, and instigate new codes because it can utilize language concretely.

Again, the reader is crucial here; to say that poetry can instigate new codes is shorthand for saying that poetry is what we call that arena of language in which readers are invited to instigate new, and often ephemeral, codes. By constructing these codes, the reader is constructing meaning, and the greater the noise in a given poem, the greater the reader's role—and the readers' resources—in constructing its meaning. Let us, just for a moment, go back to the strictly quantitative and consider poems according to a continuum of self-sufficiency. In other words, some poems seem entire on the page, with their meanings determined by the play of language within the form, while others offer impulses, directions, etc., that require extensive creative as well as interpretive activity on the part of the reader. Poems at this latter extreme assume a reader who can adapt his or her ways of reading and patterns of understanding to incorporate new material. In order for this to be possible for even the most adventurous reader, the new material cannot be entirely novel, but must work against or, more accurately, as an extension of an ambient field of meaning relationships that the reader already knows how to interpret.

This extension reflects the operation of innovation within the system of the poem itself. Any rhetorical innovation must work within a context of predictable rhetoricity, which supplies the basic code and rules of interpretation. It is, in a sense, language's memory that anchors all innovation. For instance, Keith Waldrop's lines "I would shorten my / nights by wandering my creatures"[8] can work because the syntax is normative and a connection between night and wandering has an established position in the English-language imagination; these established elements create a stable background into which a reader can fit the oddities. So, though unprecedented, the passage is read according to traditional principles, but it must also overflow those principles into others which its uniqueness spontaneously creates. The reader constructs, with these augmented principles, a parallel structure, a false double of his or her previous understanding, and superimposes it upon the first, making a passage between the two at points of resemblance, thereby gaining access to truly new elements from a point at which she or he is anchored to the conventional aspects of the text. In this way, the territories of the previously unexpressed are opened up very gradually and assimilated into a generally expanding expressive capability.

This gradual process employs a couple of techniques, differing in detail but having as a common denominator repetition and redundancy. The first time material incorporating a high degree of noise is read by a given reader, much of it will not be integrated, but will remain as a confusing background to those points of accessible meaning also present. However, with repeated readings of the same piece, slight adjustments in the reader's cognitive capability will gradually develop a structure into which the noisy elements can organize themselves; this structure will be instigated on the basis of a similarity to something familiar. Tabary has noticed the same method of adaptation in his work on organisms: "There are cases in which no preexisting schemes of conduct can reduce the noise. Then new configurations appear through combinations or modifications of preexisting configurations."[9] These modifications can begin wherever a similarity to the preexisting is perceived, whether it is syntactical, rhythmical, referential, etc. With sufficient repetition, the new element becomes ingrained, extending the permanently accessible field, and can in turn become the anchor for other extensions. On a biological level, Tabary explains: "A stimulus that constitutes noise for an inexperienced organism may be able to be neutralized easily by an organism of the same nature with greater experience."[10] Readers, though, do more than "neutralize" the noise; the reader with greater experience can actually use it to expand what can be said in a given language, and thus, what can be thought by its cultures. And it is through such a process of gradual expansion that some of what Wittgenstein termed "the inexpressible" can come close enough to language to be shown by it.

NOTES

1. This example is based on and similar to one in William Paulson, *The Noise of Culture* (Palo Alto: Stanford University Press, 1988), 72.

2. Oliver Sacks, *Awakenings* (New York: Dutton, 1983), 15.

3. Discussions of some of these applications appear in *L'auto-organisation: De la physique au politique—Colloque de Cerisy* (Paris: Éditions du Seuil, 1994).

4. Henri Atlan, *Entre le cristal et la fumée: Essai sur l'organisation du vivant* (Paris: Éditions du Seuil, 1979).

5. Jean-Claude Tabary, "Les sciences du système nerveux et le formalisme du hasard organisationnel," in *L'auto-organisation,* 246.

6. Michel Serres, *Genese* (Paris: Bernard Grasset, 1986), 32.

7. Michel Serres, "Noise," in *Sub-stance* #40 (Madison: University of Wisconsin Press, 1983), 50.

8. Keith Waldrop, *Transcendental Studies* (Berkeley: University of California Press, 2009), 65.

9. Tabary, "Les sciences du système nerveux," 262.

10. Tabary, "Les sciences du système nerveux," 246.

Bones

Mallarmé's Dice Game

It's an accepted tenet of Modernism that Mallarmé instigated a new use of the space of the page, which began in his new awareness of the page, an awareness that appreciated its physicality, and thus its status as a visual object. This awareness reflected a change in the state of poetry in the late nineteenth-century Western world. By then, poetry was irrevocably launched on its gradual shift from an art primarily heard to one primarily read. Its realm had become, perhaps for the first time ever, more the page than the open air, and its ruling sense more the eye than the ear. In response, Mallarmé truly *saw* the page; it was an object to him, not an abstract concept, not a place to score a performance occurring somewhere else. His seminal long poem *Un coup de dés*[1] acknowledges this shift and celebrates it by making the page a location, a locus of action that does not represent or record the poem, but enacts it, thus becoming a crucial aspect of it.

But *Un coup de dés* did more than establish this concrete, visible body. It also allowed a new level of ambiguity and a new mode of simultaneity to enter poetry. It caused the reader to make new and constant choices—or at least to attempt to, for often the reader's eye simply can't choose, and ends up absorbing all available possibilities. Initially, we look at his pages as we would look at a work of visual art rather than reading them as we would a more traditionally arranged page. By disrupting the visual tradition of the page, he draws our attention to the variety of stimuli that he has scattered about the surface, which means that we see this text first as a surface, first as a single thing, which we then start scanning for striking elements, immediate patterns, and discernable flow. All of this derails the default: we have not yet approached his page in the normal (to European literature) left-to-right, top-to-bottom order. And our scanning doesn't cover the page just once; it passes again and again very quickly over the surface, following different paths, accumulating ever greater detail, building in layers.

In the particular case of *Un coup de dés*, this reading strategy means that we get several poems on each spread, and that the poem as an entirety is never-ending because our active gaze is constantly rewriting it by taking its elements in different orders. Because of this, and because of the inarticulable information contained in the blank spaces that surround the language on each page, a poem such as *Un coup de dés* is even more resistant to paraphrase and more insistent on the physical reality of the word than poetry that offers relatively fewer reading options by maintaining a constant left margin and a more traditional line arrangement.

But before Mallarmé published *Un coup de dés* in 1897, we could not have spoken of "a poem such as . . . ," for *Un coup de dés* marked the first instance of a poet's treating the open two-page spread as a single unit and planning the distribution of words with not only that extension in mind, but that extension plus the inevitable gutter that would necessarily divide it in two.

And while that gutter is an abyss, a constant reminder of the *mise en abyme* that is all language, a constant reminder of the way language severs us from the world of immediate experience, it also reminds us that language and the poem are two completely different things. Like those ambiguous image pairs, such as Wittgenstein's "rabbit-duck," that we cannot see all at once, Mallarmé's gutter can suddenly flip from that negative space in language to a positive space in the poem, that of the spine. It can suddenly appear as a bold white streak stabilizing the disparate language launching out from both sides, allowing us to see that poetry has bones, that it is built on a rangy architecture of articulations that radiate outward, continually deviating from a core, managing to be somehow both ungainly and graceful.

Mallarmé's emphasis on the spine underscores the fact that poetry uses a fundamentally different mode of organization from that of prose, one arranged around a spine rather than around a line—be it a line of type, a narrative line, or a line of argument. This may seem to contradict an understanding of poetry as, more than any other genre, organized around the line, but Mallarmé, through his renovations of form, revealed a deeper layer of organization, one that pertains not to content (the line of thematic development) nor to appearance (the lines that compose the stanza), but to a more internalized and radical impulse based in the conceptual movement of poetry, which is not linear, but radiant and skeletal—it tracks a finite body, but one through which no single path will lead, creating a nonhierarchical structure composed of any number of smaller units, which may themselves include hierarchical arrangements.

The way that Mallarmé arranged the other white spaces on each spread in relation to the blazing white spine at its center often suggests an X-ray, a technology coincidentally in development just as Mallarmé was reconceiving the page. Seeing the spread as an X-ray image reinforces the parallel with the skeleton and proposes a way that white space operates in this, and increasingly in all, poetry. White space becomes the silent medium that connects and supports the more volatile, vulnerable tissue of language, even as it also becomes the absence within the sign system that connects the work to the reading body, the body that is absent from the abstraction of language, the body that recognizes itself in the skeletal white spaces.

Mallarmé's skeletons, however, are not those of balanced, symmetrical bodies, but of creatures in dynamic states of disequilibrium. And while the core constantly pulls them back, toward the center, toward the page, they thrive in that centrifugal pull, half creatures of the sea that is the abyss, half creatures of the land, standing in light. He has created these creatures so that they can survive in any extremity of mind—the chasm of the crisis of language or the grounding promise of the poem.

Ashagalomancy is an ancient practice of divination in which small bones are tossed out on the ground, and their meaning determined by the pattern they happen to form. Later, dice were used. Or it's simply a game of chance. Dice are the oldest gaming device known and were originally made of bone; "throwing bones" is an old expression for gambling, and though

I don't for a minute suppose he intended it, I can't help thinking that Mallarmé gambled a pattern of silence against the tempest of language to inaugurate an inverse signification in which white speaks, even shouts, and thus invites any and every other inverse into its intimate cartography.

NOTE

1. You can see the whole poem, with its original layout, by doing an Internet search using the title and the author's name.

Olson and the Projective

For much of Olson's career, his overarching concern was what he perceived to be the bankruptcy of Western civilization, a bankruptcy rooted in the Greco-Roman tradition of discourse, which he felt made language into a shield against actual experience. And experience, participation in the actual, was his goal. From there stemmed his emphasis on immanence, and from there, on breath, which anchored poetry's effects in physiology. His famous essay "Projective Verse" clearly lays out the poem as a field of action, as an event in process, as opposed to the model epitomized by Wordsworth's "emotions recollected in tranquility." It was not so much the emotions or the tranquility that Olson opposed, but the *re* of *recollected;* he strove for a poetry that did not represent, but that presented.

And though Olson had a healthy disdain for Western culture, it wasn't categorical; he found aspects of it quite useful, even hopeful, particularly aspects of the sciences. To advances in late nineteenth-century physics, for instance, Olson attributed the fact that man was "suddenly possessed or repossessed of a character of being, a thing among things, which I shall call his physicality."[1] And his concept of "field" is not based on the common noun, but on the Einsteinian understanding of the term as articulated by Timothy Ferris: "the domain or environment in which the real or potential action of a force can be described mathematically at each point in space."[2] Another mathematical concept he used was projective geometry, which he saw as the unifying element among a number of practices that marked the emergent art of the 1950s, including action painting and chance-based music. He stated that he took the title of his famous essay "Projective Verse" from the work of H.M.S. Coxeter on projective geometry, and Alfred North Whitehead, who was a major influence on the *Maximus Poems,* wrote a book titled *The Axioms of Projective Geometry* in 1906, though it seems that Olson didn't encounter this particular work until much later. Regardless of where he found the idea of projective geometry, he used a fairly loose definition of it. In *Muthologos,* he defines it as "that movement of force as wave and particle and particles dissolving into vibration," which has nothing to do with geometry at all. He's using metaphors based vaguely on the physics of light, the "particles" of which certainly don't dissolve—which he no doubt knew perfectly well.

Such "misuse" of scientific terminology is often taken by scientists as an affront, but there's another way to look at it, a way that reveals the poet as reaching out to scientific language for its precision, and taking it from there as raw material to be worked through metaphor, metonymy, and ambiguity until it expresses something that can't be expressed otherwise. It wasn't that Olson wanted to put poetry on a physical and therefore scientific footing; it was that he deeply believed that that was where it actually and inevitably already was.

Olson became interested in post-Euclidean geometry in the mid-1940s, and was deeply intrigued by what he understood as a completely new and more accurate way of seeing the world, one in which space is not something independent of the objects within it but is actually determined by those objects. In addition to Coxeter's work, he explored the nineteenth-century advances made by Lobachevsky, Bolyai, and Riemann, which encouraged him to think in terms of extra-dimensional space and unbounded space. There's a curious contradiction in such an intense interest in these highly abstract concepts on the part of someone as dedicated as Olson was to the immediate as revealed by the senses. But it's not so much a contradiction as an instance of Olson's recognizing a concept as a real thing in a real world, with real defined as that which has irreversible effect.

And while Olson's work couldn't take on additional dimensions in concrete terms, it did extend in space in a new way. His most radical spatial innovations occurred in *The Maximus Poems,* in some essays from the 1960s, and in his curious hybrid genre of letter/bibliography/commentary, in which we see the marks on the page straining to move beyond it by moving across it in unprecedented ways. The tension they display keeps us aware of the very real limits of our perceptions. And for one so dedicated to the actual, the increasing scientific proof of our inability to access that actual, except through the mediation of mathematics and other conceptual apparatuses, must have been extremely frustrating.

Olson applied his interest in and insight into post-Euclidean geometry in some of his critical work, such as in the essay "Equal, That Is, to the Real Itself," in which, following Riemann's categories, he draws parallels between, on the one hand, the Euclidian worldview, characterized as "discrete" ("the old system [which] includes discourse, language as it has been since Socrates"), and on the other, a post-Euclidean worldview constituting a new system that is "more true, the continuous." In short, post-Euclidean geometry reinforced the distinctions and conclusions he had developed through his more general consideration of the state of Western culture.

And it is perhaps post-Euclidean geometry in its broadest application, that of mapping extra-dimensional spaces, rather than projective geometry per se, that Olson is tapping into in much of his work, yet there are elements of projective geometry as traditionally defined that seem closely related to his projects, even though he never explicitly drew the connections.

The actual definition of projective geometry is extremely broad and somewhat elastic. Tom Clark, in his biography of Olson, takes him to task for "his inability to grasp the technical fine points," but that's a state Olson shared with all but highly advanced mathematicians—the "fine points" are, in fact, excruciatingly fine. That said, there are some basic principles that could apply particularly to his notions of projective verse, albeit taken metaphorically—and a lot rests on this distinction—i.e., can mathematical concepts be used metaphorically, or does that defeat their whole purpose? It's a hotly debated and unresolved question, but raising it, entertaining it, offers a way to explore other possibilities.

In its broadest terms, projective geometry is the geometry of projected figures (defined in one place as the geometry of a figure and all its shadows) and deals with the distortions caused by projection as well as those elements that remain invariant (for instance, a line remains a line, even though its length, and even its relationship to other lines, may have changed). So it includes, but is not limited to, the geometry of perspective, from which it might be inferred that it recognizes point of view as a determining factor of our worldview and recognizes that worldview as changeable and contingent.

Projective geometry is used in many common things; most contemporary map projections use a version of it that tries to meld the Riemannian geometry of the sphere with the demands of our two-dimensional conceptual and literal representations, and all perspective drawings use its principles. These examples employ a more basic use of the concept than Olson did, and yet the notion of his field poetics' creating a space in which the event that is the self-in-action-in-space could be projected makes a certain sense. The plane onto which the item is projected is obviously crucial to the resulting image, and poetry offers a conceptual plane flattened by convention until it's almost visible, as well as the literal, tangible space of the page. By refusing a priori poetic forms and other conventions such as the justified left margin, Olson enabled the page to receive the projection of a nuanced time as the fourth dimension in addition to the well-accepted three. More than most, Olson's poetry exists both as form in space—the page orchestrated in such a way that we see it in an instant—and also as form in time, as, like all language, it is a sequence occurring in time, and he accentuated the dynamic between these two forms through his careful use of space, which the eye must leap across, making us aware of a kind of "white time" in which the four dimensions fuse.

A projection is always a distortion that grapples across dimension, that grapples to present more dimensions than its form allows. Olson saw what could be done by activating the field of the page, but in the long run it could offer no more than an intimation, and this accurate but elusive projection is the ineffable that haunts both his ideas and his poetry, this unshakeable realization of space-time as a mundane fact, yet one we are unable to experience as such.

To say that a field poetics allows a projection of the self or of the self's experience onto the page is, of course, a metaphor.

The word "self" is itself a metaphor for an untraceable confluence of impressions and impulses; there is no figure there to
project, and the concrete mechanics of the process are completely lacking. And Olson wanted more than metaphor, which
is, I think, why he evoked the principle but then immediately
clouded it with other mathematical and physical principles that,
though related and possibly relevant, cannot be used together in
any normative fashion. The blend of these disparate terms creates an upheaval that Olson then kept up in the air, intent on
keeping the dust from settling because as long as it doesn't, the
collapse into metaphor can't occur, and intimations of an inexpressible may actually filter in through the gaps between.

Olson may have been dedicated to the immanent, actual ma-
terial-world-as-action, but the one delivered to his senses wasn't
enough. He was after a physicality that was not beyond the available but that was more intense, not a metaphysicality but a
hyper-physicality, and he looked to the language of the sciences,
but even more so to that of mathematics, for a way to collapse
the distance instigated by language. In a sense, he found the
necessary tool in numbers. Partaking of an elaborate relational
system similar to words, and like words deriving their meaning
entirely from that system, numbers nonetheless mean nothing
but themselves, *can* mean nothing but themselves, and the geometrical figures they can construct can map the physical from
the inside and emerge as the patterns of a life—not a representation of it, but the pattern itself, which can be projected, either
directly or with the distortions we've come to call the aesthetic,
onto surfaces as varied as page and planet and space.

NOTES

1. Charles Olson, *Collected Prose* (Berkeley: University of California
Press, 1997), 121.
2. Shachar Bram, *Charles Olson and Alfred North Whitehead: An Essay
on Poetry*, trans. Batya Stein (Lewisburg: Bucknell University Press,
2004), 20.

Against the Limits of Language

Geometry in the Work of Anne-Marie Albiach and Susan Howe

> Man has the urge to thrust against the limits of
> language . . . But the tendency, the thrust, *points to
> something.*
>
> —Ludwig Wittgenstein

Wittgenstein does not say what this *something* is, and similarly, the many writers whose work today tries to stretch the boundaries of the sayable through the manipulation of various elements do not necessarily state, or even care, what they're pushing toward; what they care about is the possibility that there is something beyond language and to which, paradoxically, only language can bring us.

The interest is not new; Rosmarie Waldrop, for one, has traced its history through Western writing in her book *Against Language?* In her study, she demonstrates that experimental poetry—poetry that works through altering or distorting language—is historically engaged with a notion of the inherent insufficiency of language and with a fascination for its amorphous boundaries.

Wittgenstein addressed this question from another angle in the *Tractatus Logico-Philosophicus,* 3.262. His statement "What does not get expressed in the sign is shown by its application" points to a region of meaning that can't be captured in language and that yet can be sensed. His use of the word "shown," though it has a host of additional implications, in this context resonates with J. L. Austin's concept of performative language, which is based on the conviction that while some, even most, language uses operate referentially, others actually accomplish or actualize something. For instance, the words "I now pronounce you husband and wife," which close the traditional Christian wedding ceremony, not only refer to an abstract relationship, but actually bring about its legal correlate. To quote another of Austin's examples, the sentence "I bet you'll win the race" is referential language until it's accompanied by a ten-dollar bill or some other wagered item, in which case it becomes performative because the phrase "I bet" is an act as well as a statement. As Austin increasingly conceded, all language use has its performative aspects, slighter in some cases, stronger in others.

The conjunction of the referential and the performative—that point at which reference and action, representation and presentation, begin to fuse—is the most promising site for an expansion of language into previously inarticulable territory, and writing constructed as an act entire on the page is always in part pushing into that territory.

Two contemporary writers, Anne-Marie Albiach and Susan Howe, focus on the page as an active stage, using geometry to facilitate their projects of reconfiguration and expansion. Both bodies of work can be mapped in many ways; considering them from the perspective of fractal geometry offers a reading that displays the unusual kind of motion that drives these works and enables them to elicit fresh meaning from familiar language.

Fractal geometry caught the public imagination some twenty years ago because of the vivid pictures it could spawn on computer screens and the metaphoric wealth it offered. As a mathematical concept, fractal geometry was popularized by Benoît Mandelbrot, beginning with the first publication of his book *Les Objets fractals* in 1975. As Mandelbrot himself asserts, he did not "discover" the phenomenon;[1] its historical development dates back to the beginning of the twentieth century in the work of Jean Perrin and Felix Hausdorff. However, prior to Mandelbrot's work, the paradigm had remained within the realm of pure mathematics, with the exception of Perrin's early work and Norbert Wiener's later work on Brownian motion. Mandelbrot extended the application of fractal geometry by showing that it could be directly and usefully applied to a more complete understanding of various natural forms.

As Mandelbrot also asserts, the basic idea is both simple and concrete.[2] The now well-known figure of the von Koch snowflake offers a particularly accessible example, and you can find it easily by doing an Internet search using "von Koch snowflake" as the key words. In short, you begin with an equilateral triangle, and use the middle third of each side as the base of another equilateral triangle, which gives you a Star of David, upon which you perform the same function, using each middle third as the base of another triangle, which results in a form sometimes seen in Arabic tile art. If you perform the same function again to each line segment, the result is a figure that begins to resemble a snowflake. Given infinitely precise tools, you could continue to perform this function infinitely, making the resulting line infinite in length, yet the form will never exceed a circle drawn to touch the three points of the original triangle. It's the paradox of an infinite line within a finite space that gives the form its fractional dimension: it is more than a line and less than a plane. The dimension of this particular form is 1.26.

As a lens on literature, fractal geometry's forms are not as useful as the peculiar type of motion that they embody. This motion is based in part on the role that the fractal plays as a "third term." Mandelbrot himself described the form as mediating between two poles in such a way as to create something new: "between the domain of uncontrolled chaos and the excessive order of Euclid, there is from now on a new zone of fractal order."[3] In literature also, the fractal offers an opening onto a space between the utterly unstructured and structures whose fixity restricts the possibilities of the language they support. It creates such a space between extremes by creating a pattern along which a mediation can be articulated. This new form is neither a third pole nor a compromise between (combination or rearrangement of elements of) the two original poles; rather, it is something new that breaks up a binary entrenchment by stepping outside of its terms.

Thus the nature of the fractal form is not static, but transformative. The term "fractal object" implies an object that is fissuring infinitely; therefore, there is no possible "final" or rested state for it to attain. Any image of a fractal object is an artificially arrested version of the real (though abstract) object, which is, of course, impossible to reproduce. Such an image is analogous to a photograph of a person: a body is never that still, but representing it as such can have its uses. This can be equally applied to language, with a word seen as the snapshot, the artificial stoppage of the ongoing motion of meaning.

The motion of meaning is a fractal motion, infinitely complicating itself along a pattern of self-similarity. However, unlike the determined and symmetrical von Koch snowflake, linguistic meaning can incorporate infinite variations and is invaded by chance, making it more analogous to Brownian motion. Brownian motion is the erratic motion traced by microscopic particles in suspension; you can find an image of a path traced by that motion by doing an Internet search using "Brownian motion" as the key words.

A magnified fragment of this path would look just like the entire image you saw; in other words, like all fractals, it shows self-similarity across scale, which is to say that any fragment of it looks just like the whole. The more you magnified any portion of it, the more detail it would reveal, and that detail, given infinitely fine equipment, would reveal itself to be infinite. Thus the "line" between any points A and B on the path, while always spanning a finite space, is infinite in length. Its principle is the same as that of the von Koch curve, except that it incorporates random elements rather than developing deterministically. In other words, while the random elements send its development in unpredictable directions, they do not affect its basic properties of self-similarity across scale, infinite expansion within a finite space, and spanned dimension. As a motion without end, it is eternally becoming.

Reading the work of both Howe and Albiach according to a fractal model subtly expands the signifying potential of their language. This model also offers a reading in which these works have no beginnings or endings, but maintain open forms that both emphasize the self-sufficiency of the page and expand beyond it. While neither writer claims an interest in specifically fractal geometry, both consciously and frequently allude to geometry in a general sense as a way of addressing the problematic of space. For instance, Susan Howe's book *Pythagorean Silence* evokes the field in its very title. Pythagoras, often considered the first geometer, is credited with having taken mathematics from the purely practical to the realm of the theoretical, the philosophical. And as geometry is concerned with the definition, construction, and possibilities of space, it is fitting that the project at the base of this book and of much of her early work is one of respatialization, of reconfiguring the space of the page so that it is no longer controlled by the linear progression so habitual to written language. Howe does this quite dramatically in some of her work, by overlapping diagonal lines or arranging words in an orchard pattern, making a vertical or diagonal reading as logical as a horizontal one. Many of the pages in *Pythagorean Silence* operate just as radically, but more subtly, presenting a difference in their motion as well as in their appearance by replaying the book's principal themes and references at various scales in a way that does not advance them and does not depend on an accumulation of what has come before. For instance, one theme present at the level of the entire book is that of the crucial role of language in problematizing presence, a theme that is captured succinctly at the level of the phrase in lines such as "I cannot / call presence and in its / absence / fold in one hand // *what*".[4] The theme is neither advanced nor resolved; we do not move from one element to another in an accumulative fashion, but instead endlessly return, for accumulation and resolution are not the goals; instead, as the theme has announced, it is presence itself that is at stake, and calling it into being is sufficient but never conclusive; it must constantly be reenacted.

Howe interweaves several themes throughout this book, enacting them at the level of the phrase, the line, the page, the sequence, and the book itself; thus a phrase may have the same relationship to the page as the page has to the book, the whole showing self-similarity across scale. Furthermore, many of her themes are presented as paradoxes, which allows her to play with binary opposition in a way that produces a third term that is not a synthesis, but, like the middle third in the Koch curve, becomes an equal partner, dimensionally expanding the unit. One paradoxical pair that recurs throughout the text is forgetting and memory. It emerges in lines such as "Recollection returns / forgotten Boundless,"[5] which, in the paradox of the "boundless return," itself implies a kind of fractal motion. However, as with most of her paradoxical pairs, this one is not constant, for the notion of forgetting is also played off against knowledge and knowing; thus, the opposition is not a closed pair, but an open and generative one.

Sound also moves through this book along fractal patterns. Off-rhyme, sometimes mixed with alliteration, creates slightly ajar correspondences that propel the reader backwards and forwards through a given passage, so that while the habits of reading send attention forward, sound and spacing cause that same attention to ricochet about, gathering meaning, but not progressively. Such sound use creates a geometry of unclosable elements because the second term, just slightly ajar or displaced, includes something extra, a remainder, a new element that operates as an opening to invite still other terms into an endlessly self-productive equation. But it's not a progressive production or a resolvable equation; rather, the structures set up a field of relationships that both augment and compromise each other.

> Farewel—
> twin half torn to pearl
>
> not a sparrow
>
> shall fall[6]

In the passage above, "Farewel" rhymes with "sparrow" in its first syllable (but obliquely because of their varied stresses), while its second syllable interacts with "pearl" both in the final *l* and in the vowel sounds; those of "pearl" are a condensed version of those of "farewel." The *r* around which the word "pearl" collects performs the same function in "sparrow," while the words "shall fall" establish links with what preceded them through repeating the final *l,* as well as composing a concise off-rhyme in themselves. The next line, which belongs, thematically, to another section, yet includes the word "shadow," which links its resonant field with this one above. Another example:

> power of vision   a vast
> zero
>
> or zest for action[7]

Here, the sounds form an odd equation in which vision ÷ vast = action (the v's and the s's canceling each other out), but, as always, the equation is an open one, for "vast" is also communicating with "zest," which is, in turn, communicating with "zero." These relationships prevent the reader's attention from proceeding in a single direction; instead, it follows an intricate and indeterminate path among the varied elements. The word "erratic" a few lines later functions like the "shadow" cited above, forming a bridge between thematic fields. The bridging insures that no field or passage is readable as closed; each one pivots into the one following, which in turn refers to the one preceding. As soon as a figure is established, it is reconstructed, and, as above, the reconstruction takes place at the level of the page, the passage, and the phrase. No matter at what scale the sound activity is examined, the same patterning is revealed.

Not only does the fractal paradigm direct the movement of this piece, but it also appears indirectly in the content. The phrase quoted above is one example—"Recollection returns / forgotten Boundless"—and there as others, such as:

> The measure of force
> (as magnitude) as fixed
>
> in flux[8]

The words "fixed // in flux" in particular are evocative of the fractal figure's peculiar property of infinite expansion that cannot exceed a fixed boundary. The same notion appears more strongly as an aspect of spatialization in the lines "Some particular place fleeting // and fixed."[9]

Susan Howe's respatialization also uses absence in an expansive way, for though an emphasis on the material world and its concrete objects distinguishes her work, she's also very interested in what lies between concrete objects. These betweens are Pythagoras's silences; they reign over the unmapped and unbounded zones between delineated forms, the territory of the unsayable stretching between well-worn words: "This is one reason the entrance of *space* into the lines is so important—that space is what cannot be said."[10] These spaces, these betweens, once established, are kept in motion, maintained as active aspects of the poem by the fractal activity of the words around them so that both known and unexplored territories are continually expanding.

2

The work of the French poet Anne-Marie Albiach, a contemporary of Howe's, makes use of fractal geometry in surprisingly similar ways. Many of her pages show the quality of self-similarity across scale, such as the following:

WHO ACCOMPANIES HIM

> which of the two
> will emerge the most
> affected through
> difference

*It appears as the first
legend:*

the one forever elaborating the Reflection,

each eye a separate look

and
"for some years now"

SACRILEGE AND SACRIFICE: Unknowing

In the bodily fold of
scandal

ECHO
:there are
many of them[11]

Everything that is said in the book is also said on this page, but in a unique way. If broken down further, many of its individual phrases would also reflect the book's principal themes: "the one forever elaborating the Reflection" or "In the bodily fold of / scandal" or "ECHO / :there are / many of them"—each of these phrases, in its own way, sums up the book as a whole, and yet the book as a whole is not an accumulative structure; it is instead a single gesture, or rather, a snapshot stopping a gesture in midmotion, a gesture whose constituent parts all replicate themselves. Whereas most books move progressively from beginning to end, their last pages indicating either closure or, if left open, the continuation of a progression in some unspecified space, each of Albiach's books ends at a final page that does not resolve previously established issues or send the reader on to another text; instead, her last pages continue to develop the themes, as on previous pages, sending us back to them.

Throughout each of her books, the fragmentations of the lines are such that one can open the book anywhere and begin; one will always be beginning in the middle, and in the middle of a movement. The movement is primary and perpetual; it is entire in the sense that it dissolves all-that-might-move into the motion itself, yet the poem goes nowhere. Instead, the movement occurs within a described space; it is nonfinite in its complexifying bifurcations and incorporations, yet it can never exceed its initial boundary.

Throughout Albiach's work, direct reference to geometry is always ambiguous, but, equally, always central. The second line of one of her principal books reads, "In the power of his geometric statements, he has perhaps established it at right angle to the irreversible."[12] Her work deals not with an abstract and philosophical space, but with the immanent space of the human body as confused with and/or fused with the space of the page. The mapping of the human body and the role that language plays in positioning that body is a recurrent theme, inviting questions of materiality at a level both intimate and universal, which in turn raises a question about the real distance between such levels:

> he accepts the circle, speech and so
> resolves himself
> is reabsorbed into a higher equation
>
> IRREDUCIBLE GEOMETER[13]

Albiach also uses binary pairs, playing with the possibility of dialectical progression, but, as in the passage above, a synthetic resolution is always finally denied: the geometer is neither "he" nor "the circle, speech"; it is the ambiguous and irreducible release from the dialectic; it is the agent aspect of geometry, used not as a metaphor, but as an accurate enactment of a moment of relationship. Her geometry is an unbounded and flexible construction in which she activates a system of numerous oppositional pairs—body/text, male/female, presence/absence, dark/light, text/white space—and then denies their opposition by keeping them in constant mutation, splitting and recombining them in various ways. For instance, body is at times opposed to text, which is then in turn opposed to white space; in other instances, body is opposed to voice, which is then opposed to silence or to text.

While all her pairs are in constant motion and interaction, their interactions never deliver compromise, combination, or cancellation; they result instead in excess—in a third term that is not a product of the first two, but that has a nature of its own. The end of the poem "CAESURA: *the body*"[14] addresses this process directly, using her principal pair—body of being/body of text:

repetition
"the body bears the white space of the fiction that divides it"

---

and becomes this excess:

This motion is, again, similar to that of the Koch snowflake—a third and "between" term drops out and is paired off, creating a new opposition. Following such a motion, Albiach never covers new ground, but expands indefinitely within her established boundaries. She is, in a sense, mining the depth of a surface—the defining paradox of fractal motion.

GEOMETRY

they open
in retreat [15]

Motion is a central aspect of meaning in language and is usually taken for granted, as it is so often the same linear, unidirectional, and accumulative motion. By relying on a different type of motion, in this case fractal, both of these writers establish new relationships among familiar words, relationships that jolt the reading mind into new sensations and perceptions. It's work that continually reminds us of the importance of relationship, the active, even energetic tissue that, in turn, activates words grown sluggish in their stability.

NOTES

1. Benoit B. Mandelbrot, *The Fractal Geometry of Nature* (New York: W. H. Freeman, 1983), introduction (passim).

2. Ibid.

3. Ibid., 10.

4. Susan Howe, *The Europe of Trusts* (Los Angeles: Sun & Moon Press, 1990), 24.

5. Ibid., 59.

6. Ibid., 26.

7. Ibid., 31.

8. Ibid., 65.

9. Ibid., 71.

10. Susan Howe, letter to the author. March, 1994.

11. Anne-Marie Albiach, *Mezza Voce,* trans. Joseph Simas et al. (Sausalito: Post-Apollo Press, 1988), 48.

12. Ibid., 15.

13. Anne-Marie Albiach, *Etat,* trans. Keith Waldrop (Windsor, VT: Awede Press, 1989), 97.

14. Albiach, *Mezza Voce,* 121–36.

15. Ibid., 152–53.

Seeing Reading

Susan Howe's Moving Margins

"Why read?"—I heard this question put forth the other night by someone who is both a poet and a literature professor. In the context of the discussion at hand, it meant, "Why are we continuing to base education on reading? Is there any real advantage to reading as opposed to getting information from DVDs, videos, films, or other media?" In short, why do we, as a culture, privilege reading—in theory, at least, if not in practice? Reading is generally considered an "intellectual" activity, thus "worthy," while watching TV, for instance, is considered lazy—why?

It's a good question, and I was surprised by how many answers came to mind over the next few weeks. The first but perhaps the most enduring thought was that reading is unique because of the verbal-visual fusion it demands; this is fundamental to reading, and it *is* something, it *does* something; it makes something happen in the brain that has a physiological effect.

Words on a page, or on any other surface, constitute a different event, on the one hand, from words presented audibly, and on the other, from other lines and forms that could appear on a sheet of paper or other two-dimensional surface. Poetry amounts to a particularly heightened instance of this event because, with its attention to line break and page space, it accentuates the visual aspect while, with its equal emphasis on sound relationships such as rhyme, rhythm, and alliteration, it also accentuates the oral, thus equally engaging our two main senses, seeing and hearing. Furthermore, poetry that works to maximize these two modes can deliver an experience that is 100 percent aural and 100 percent visual, which results in an overload, an overflow, which spills into another zone of perception, creating an active hybrid between the two senses. And it is above all the "between" itself that is created and that is full of cultural and creative promise.

"Betweens" are a particular focus of Susan Howe's work, and she activates them both within the poems and through their margins, using them to work toward a fusion of perceptions. Howe's interest in "betweens" is apparent in her titles, which often focus on gaps or boundaries or bridges:

Hinge Picture
The Western Borders
Secret History of the Dividing Line
Speeches at the Barriers
Singularities
Frame Structures

Each of these evokes an edge, a limit, a spatial definition that is in some way articulated, or connected, and in each case, the connection itself is given more weight than the elements it connects. *Secret History of the Dividing Line*,[1] for instance, focuses entirely on the line of division, saying nothing about what is being divided. Parameters have greater importance for Howe than do the areas they define. A margin is a kind of parameter, but a very particular kind in that it not only defines an area, but also constitutes its own separate space. It's the dividing line made extra-dimensional, inhabitable.

Margins, as the articulations between text and world, are crucial sites for writers. The word "margins" dates back to the fourteenth-century Middle English *mergyns* and is derived from the Latin *marginibus*,[2] which means edge, border, frontier, and is related to the word "march," as in "to walk in a stately, deliberate manner."[3] So, while margins carry implications of the out-of-bounds, beyond the organizations and restrictions of the spaces they enclose, constituting a space in which one not only can but must create one's own version of order, they also necessarily include an unsettled quality, a restlessness that is nonetheless patterned, thus offering order without stasis, which embodies a model transitional zone, which margins always are. Margins negotiate not only the transition from the ordered to the random, but also that from the symbolic or the ideal to the actual;

they are the air-lock through which the distance of writing step-by-step becomes the immediacy of lived experience.

Though today, for the most part, they are intended to be ignored, margins have an intricate and active history. They developed in the Middle Ages as text and ornament became increasingly separate. Consider, for instance, the highly worked "carpet" pages of the *Book of Kells* or the *Lindisfarne Gospel,* in which text and ornament are fused. These images can easily be found by doing an Internet search using the titles. In them, each letter is an ornament in itself and is woven into the background to create a single visual object. Any empty space around it is not a border, but is instead the field in which it sits, and therefore has a different relationship to the visual/text object. But as the book became increasingly less a visual exaltation of the text and more an aid to remembering it and a score for reciting or performing it, the text became simpler and clearer. Margins aided this clarity, as well as making the book easier to hold when reading from it. And with margins, came marginalia.

In the high Middle Ages, margins were the place for gloss and commentary on texts recognized as finalized, as fixed (as opposed to interlinear glosses, which were used on texts considered in progress or in some other way less rigidly set). Yet, the effect of a marginal gloss was precisely to "unfix" the text, to keep it in the mill of reconstitution, suggesting an early recognition that with a book came the danger of a text's becoming static, going into a metaphoric rigor mortis. Marginalia, by casting doubt, adding detail, and presenting alternatives, brought a text to life again.

For Susan Howe, margins still serve this reanimating function, but that's not the only thing they do. They also function as the physical mark of silence, recording its weight, a function in turn related to the larger political and cultural question of marginalization. The force and role of the silenced is a question that has surfaced again and again in post–World War II innovative art. Within this large field, Howe often chooses to focus specifically on the issue of women's positions and women's writing, as well as on the marginalization of cultural production—especially poetry—in the United States.

Though her focus is determined, it is not direct; it's primarily through formal elements such as the margin that she enacts rather than addresses these concerns. She activates the margin in a "corner of the eye" sense, exploiting the odd acuity of peripheral vision, with its peculiar sensitivity to motion. In addition to these rather abstract, symbolic, and/or metaphoric functions, Howe uses margins immediately and concretely as a counterweight to certainty; they are the necessary ballast for words, the white ambiguity against which the definitive black of ink can be heard/seen, and that constantly throws the latter into doubt. At the same time, the margins control the text, hem it in, give it shape, and prevent it from dissipating, from merging seamlessly with the world.

As blank spaces inviting writing, margins are the physical and persistent assertion of potential. They're an invitation to the reader to respond to the book, which is to carry it on into the future. They incite the reader to talk back, to differ, to underscore, to amend. Suddenly, not only is the text destabilized, but also the reader is no longer passive, and is instead recast as an active respondent. The margin is a clinamen, disrupting equilibrium.

And most important in Howe's case, her intentional use of the margin—and of white space wherever it occurs—emphasizes the visual reality of the page. It is not simply a score for a performance somewhere else; it's a visual composition in its own right. Her white space is positive space, "pale and bright,"[4] a source of light.

The pages of *Hinge Picture*, an early book from 1974, which is reproduced in *Frame Structures*,[5] offer good illustrations. In many cases, the margins are determining factors—they establish line length, and thus control the line breaks as well as the patterns of breath and the rhythm at which the images and ideas unfold. You can see the first couple of pages on Google Books; do an Internet search for the book and then go to pages 33 and 34 in the book itself. These offer good examples, but if you have access to a copy, page 46 offers a particularly dramatic example. On the top half of that page, the margins truly dominate—they are so wide that they are literally "on the verge" of squeezing out the text all together. They are taking over; soon the margin will be the content itself. And on all the pages, the margins create a strong, visual element, holding the text to a shape.

However, predominant margins do not necessarily indicate pressure; on the contrary, some of her texts seem to wallow in their margins, or to be overwhelmed by or cast adrift among their margins, while others simply stroll about, at home in them—whatever the case, the margin is always at least as active in determining this state as is the block of text itself. In fact, of course, they can't be discussed separately, or in any way separated; margin and text always construct each other, and Howe's work underscores this point. Often, her margin/text relationships approach a classical elegance, echoing the generous standard set by William Morris in his work on book design at the end of the nineteenth century, which in turn has roots that go back to the early days of the codex. Morris's work in part posits grace as an equilibrium between light and dark spaces, a gyroscopical pause and suspension—like a sneeze; anything can enter.

Howe's text "Melville's Marginalia," which appears in *The Non-conformist's Memorial*,[6] and is based on the notes that Melville made in the margins of the books he owned, offers another way of entering into her own margins. Her choosing this text amounts to choosing to write marginalia on marginalia, and thus to add another margin to the margin, which suggests that a page can expand indefinitely. (A suggestion realized when you find yourself making notes in the margins of Howe's *Melville's Marginalia* . . .) The text itself remains fairly marginal to its title, concentrating principally on the life, works, and notes of James Clarence Mangan, a marginal mid-nineteenth-century Irish writer who, Howe feels, was or should or could have been the prototype of that master of obsessive self-marginalization, Bartleby.

In this text, the margin takes on a body; it begins to wander both in the form of Mangan himself and in the notion of ghosts. Howe's evocation and use of ghosts is very different from her references to the dead. Ghosts are neither living nor dead, and so offer a third state, one whose territory is the periphery. And here the periphery is not so much a relative position as it is a different quality, requiring different senses, such as a different kind of seeing. Ghosts are primary among the things seen more clearly with the corner of the eye, and like that entire class of entities, they are most easily seen when moving. Ghosts function as the insistent invitation to alter; they are the constant presence of the undiscovered. In this text, ghostliness is linked not only to Mangan's wandering, but also to his pseudonymity—"Ah, you know not what a vagabond I am," writes Mangan;[7] "under so many pseudonyms," writes the *Encyclopedia Britannica*.[8] Anonymity, nomadism, and incorporeality are all versions of the animated margin.

The dead, on the other hand, seem to occupy another zone similar in quality to our own and have nothing to do with margins per se; if they seem to, it's only because the margin is the one place we can encounter them, as if the margin in this case amounted to the overlapping extremes of two exclusive but similar worlds: "Marks he made in the margins of his books are often a conversation with the dead,"[9] Howe states at the beginning of *Melville's Marginalia*—which gets further interfolded by Howe's own act of "conversing" with the now-dead interlocutor of the dead.

The dead and their relationship to margins come up again in the introduction to a more recent book, *Pierce-Arrow*.[10] In the course of musing about microform, she comments, "It is strange how the dead appear in dreams where another space provides our living space as well. Another language another way of speaking so quietly always there in the shape of memories, thoughts, feelings, which are extra-marginal outside of primary consciousness, yet must be classed as some sort of unawakened finite infinite articulation."[11] She makes an equation here between the extra-marginal and an entity that is simultaneously three equally "other-ed" elements—space, language, and way of speaking. It is their fusion, or rather, their shared identity, that constitutes the added marginal dimension. The nature of that dimension is potentiality, and its articulation, the promise of ever-imminent connection.

The margin as a formal and metaphoric element is a key theme throughout *Pierce-Arrow*, which is centered on Charles Peirce and his wife, Juliette, both of whom were marginal people in their own ways. Juliette was of undetermined and (in the eyes of their neighbors) "marginal" background (most likely at least half gypsy), while Peirce was of indeterminate character, volatile, drunken, and licentious. Their examples point out that indeterminacy is as fundamental a quality of the marginal as is eccentricity. Perhaps not surprisingly, the couple found themselves marginalized by late nineteenth-century polite New York society. But in keeping with the habits of the marginal yet mobile, the couple that was exiled from society a hundred years ago has (like Mangan) now found its way to the center of a particularly edgy and incisive text.

Margins that refuse to stay on the margins, that take advantage of their restless natures and roam about—Howe enacts them in one of her frequently used stanzaic forms, her single-line stanzas separated by large spaces, which are, themselves, margins, such as appear throughout *The Europe of Trusts*,[12] which collects several early works. In these cases, the margin has completely infiltrated the text; it has interleaved itself with the center, becoming itself central without becoming any less marginal. The form implies that there's always an unsaid to unsettle everything said, a silence to parallel every utterance.

This internal margin occurs in the content also, in brief double inversions, such as the phrase "twin half torn" from *Pythagorean Silences* (see the longer passage in the essay "Against the Limits of Language"), in which, through paradox, she locates limits and frontiers within the text itself, revealing an outside within that text, a wilderness that continues coincidently with the order of printed language, a gap that suddenly gapes and then seals back up again.

These gaps are important to her, as she makes clear on the back of *Pierce-Arrow:* "It's the blanks and gaps that to me actually represent what poetry is—the connections between seemingly unconnected things—as if there is a place and might be a map to thought, when we know there is not." In defining gaps as "the connections between seemingly unconnected things," she effectively claims that a gap is not an emptiness, but an active coupling. In addition, the phrase "the connections between seemingly unconnected things" reveals a huge leap of faith, a faith in history—a faith that history might eventually and inventively make some other sense, that there might be connections. The phrase also underscores the fact that connection, in this late-postmodern moment, is becoming more and more equivalent to meaning. Howe demonstrates that serendipity is not frivolous, but fundamental and functional, and that contingency allows each thing to remain itself, enriched by association with other things, and conforming to a meaning model opposed to the metaphorically based one in which meaning is achieved through paraphraseability or exchangeability.

The phrase "as if there is a place and might be a map to thought, when we know there is not" suggests the effort of artifice, the exploration of the lie of the what-is-not—and the mapping of it. Can the "not" be mapped? Why not? It would amount to creating it—to positively asserting a negative space. The nonzone of the gap between is the obvious place for such a construction. Her use of the word "map" is important too, for a map is, like her own work, both read and seen; it makes the visual vie with the verbal, presenting words in a nonlinear order.

Though Howe's work always questions the line between the visual and the verbal, *Pierce-Arrow* plays with it in a particularly marked way through her use of Peirce's manuscripts. An Internet search using "*Pierce-Arrow*" as a key word will let you access some of these manuscript pages in the Google Books version. When pages of his original manuscript appear, they are often facing a text page of her own, so we are forced to notice that, though there are strong visual similarities, we treat them differently. Do we read the Peirce? Do we see the Howe? When we encounter either, their ambiguous natures cause us to do something in-between, but soon the mind tends to choose one of the two approaches. Choosing to read the Peirce would mean turning it into a temporal event, resolving the simultaneous impact of the visual into a series of stimuli that follow in a determinate chain. And, choosing to see the Howe would amount to the inverse—turning it into a spatial event, appreciating the entirety as a whole, rather than in the time-release fashion occasioned by reading.

Howe's work, through its use of margins and other visual, formal devices, always puts us on the borderline between these two modes of perception, and she does so intentionally, keeping us there as long as possible, creating structures that help us resist choosing. It's a vertiginous resistance because we hang suspended over her gap. And in that suspension, something new happens, something that is neither reading nor seeing, or rather, something that makes reading seeing, and that makes apparent aspects of the work that themselves span the two poles and that therefore remain invisible most of the time. We feel it as a little click in the head, something that leaps and that lands on another side, creating it.

NOTES

This title intentionally echoes that of Stephen Ratcliffe's collection of essays *Listening to Reading* (Albany: State University of New York Press, 2000).

1. Susan Howe, *Secret History of the Dividing Line* (New York: Telephone Books, 1979).

2. *Oxford English Dictionary* (Oxford: Oxford University Press, 2010).

3. See http://dictionary.reference.com/browse/margin.

4. Susan Howe, *The Non-Conformist's Memorial* (New York: New Directions, 1993), 118.

5. Susan Howe, *Frame Structures* (New York: New Directions, 1996).

6. Howe, *Non-conformist's Memorial.*

7. Ibid., 104.

8. Ibid., 109.

9. Ibid., 89.

10. Susan Howe, *Pierce-Arrow* (New York: New Directions, 1999).

11. Ibid., 6.

12. Susan Howe, *The Europe of Trusts* (New York: New Directions, 2002).

The Infinite Mountain

Nicolas Pesquès

Nicolas Pesquès has been writing a single poem for thirty years. In a way, it's a poem about endlessness, about inexhaustibility, the inexhaustibility of the earth and of affection. In clipped, enigmatic phrases, he explores the intricate and innumerable connections between man and world. Through the seven books it comprises to date, he has constructed an internal landscape that reflects the sensuousness and spirit of the mountain he sees from his window. While this internal landscape is not language itself, it is entirely constructed by language used in such a way as to constitute both a recognition and an extension of all that cannot be said. And as such, it can never end.

La face nord de Juliau[1] is a serial work, and thus has a fundamentally different shape from most poetry, and instead finds its natural links with serial works in other media from painting to dance, for the shape, in this case, overrides the medium. The impulse to seriality is an impulse toward completeness equipped with an uncommonly, and debilitatingly, astute understanding of perspective, which acknowledges it as always contingent and always, at least theoretically, changeable. Seriality recognizes that such contingency and changeability make a series at once both impossible and inexhaustible. Seriality is an impulse, not for progress, but for a more distilled kind of motion, or for process purely and sheerly, process in which nothing is produced but the process itself.

Which is a statement that, seven books later, risks sounding absurd: there is certainly something rather than nothing here; there is a tangible, traceable product, yet on another level, the pure process that is seriality demands an undoing precisely reciprocal to its doing. Pesquès has achieved this reciprocity through his relentless accumulation of a material so light it dissipates before it precipitates. In his evocation of presences, he has concentrated on the most delicate—sheer color. In earlier volumes, it was green; then it became increasingly, and is now entirely, yellow. At times this yellow is attached to physical things, most often to plants, most often to the English broom that covers the mountain, but equally frequently, and more deftly, with more difficulty, it is not attached at all. Yellow ascends, suspends, floats off, takes on a life of its own. A color so freed becomes an attractive force; it pulls things—sensations, memories, desires—to it, magnetic. So, on the one hand, we have the ghosts of its prior attachments, ineradicable, and on the other, the myriad things that leap to complete the association: butter, utter, sun. And off on a gleaming chain. Once freed from things, color can become pure adjective and pure adverb. With yellow it is brief, it is fleet. Like the flowers of the vivid broom, it has a scent and a fragility that keep time always in the foreground of all its relationships (which perfectly complements seriality, which also is always wrestling with time because it is so dedicated to refuting it, to reenacting the act of re-beginning, to refusing to count by counting only its own instances; in a true series, every item is numbered 1).

Back to yellow: it has a history of intensity. It is light. Light under tremendous pressure. Light solidified, embodied, turned to a living thing. By mining this vibrant attribute at the expense of its attachments, by mining yellow with less and less attention to *things that are* yellow, Pesquès annexes that intensity and unleashes its errancy; yellow is allowed to circulate freely, to penetrate and to expand, appearing in various forms and directions, all ephemeral. Ephemerality is key to Pesquès's project, pointing us toward the ephemeral nature of time and space—the quick passing of the seasons and the extreme fragility of the earth. By focusing on the earth's fragility in one of its most monumental forms, we are struck by the force of paradox: inevitable erosion and eternal beauty; what we see before our eyes and what lives on in the eye of the mind.

Turning vivid physical entities into charged linguistic intricacies is one of the principal mechanisms of Pesquès's poem, and is the one that keeps his system of land and language from ever becoming metaphorical. Metaphor is always an act of replacement, and as such, a gesture of identity, yet Pesquès's work intentionally mixes the terms of both fields to insist on their simultaneous primacy and essentiality: they cannot stand in or stand for one another; each is sovereign, and their relation is real. They are two irreducible elements negotiating their common space, their common responsibility.

That said, through his light, oblique touch, Pesquès delicately (con)fuses land and language into a landscape that gives us the opportunity to watch our own minds at work. Behind his terse, trim phrases, there is often an intricate turn of thought exploring the ways that language imprisons us, on the one hand, and liberates us on the other:

> *writing would then*
> *be able to account*
> *beyond the cut*
> *for that from which*
> *he who writes*
> *is himself split*[2]

Disrupting the raw immediacy of our perceptions, distancing us permanently from an unmediated immersion in our own lives, language nonetheless offers us another life of resonant connections and reverberating linings, echoes, and parallels. Pesquès pinpoints the ironic fact that language's rich gift of this other world is our only mode of exploring the world that language severs us from. He evokes this, in part, by focusing on the struggle between presence and absence in which language is inevitably engaged and that forms the texture and dynamic of his work. He struggles alongside language to burst into inevitability, to stand not for something, but simply to *stand*, to stand up to the world and to be sufficient to it.

Before him, there is a mountain. It has, despite erosion, both actually and symbolically, a constancy achieved by few things in life—memory, maybe; desire, perhaps—but the persistence of a mountain underscores the fugitive nature of anything human. Yet can a writer, by tracking the continual, infinitesimal, and ultimately crucial changes in such a monumental constant, slowly reconstruct that constancy, that cruciality, within? To build a land within is perhaps the larger, vaguer project behind any written thing—not to build a world, but to build a landscape, which is to say, not abstract in any way—only what you can see, a true extension, an unfurling that is liberating in the way that only a view can be, as it allows the body to extend itself through an overflow of the senses. As Pesquès's work shows us, writing is the sixth sense, a sense unleashed by the overflow of all the rest, and the one that allows the other five to extend beyond the self.

Pesquès has at times referred to Cezanne's relationship to Mont Saint-Victoire to talk about the inexhaustibility that the serial structure guarantees. The unique work of art, be it painted, written, or dreamed, is instantly sealed, a sovereign object that becomes immediately historical. If it is repeated once, it gains a doppelganger, a sosie, the mirror, the ventriloquist, all the multivalent ways of being not-exactly-similar, yet, as with a mirror, the system remains a closed one. But if the gesture of repetition is repeated a second time, it ignites a generating machine capable of finding infinite degrees of difference and more and more differentiating criteria: color, form, shape, line, tone, tint, silhouette, temperature. Pesquès's series declared itself as such with the first book through its serial repetition of images, and each subsequent text has necessitated the next through a constant evolution of imagery and theme. It is a series that has at its center a "strange attractor," a single point back to which its line of inquiry, its line of errancy, always returns while never tracing quite the same route back to it. This point is a mountain, and if Borges is right and infinity is actual, this route to it will eventually touch upon everything, all the details of an infinitely rich world, and then begin to invent more of them through its traveling. *La face nord de Juliau* creates a continuous line ever extending in the form of this constant return.

NOTES

1. Nicolas Pesquès, *La face nord de Juliau 1–7* (Paris: Dimanche Editeur, 1988–2010).

2. Pesquès, *La face nord de Juliau 6*, 57.

Peter Gizzi's City
The Political Quotidian

Since Whitman and Baudelaire, the everyday has increasingly been the territory of modern poetry. It amounts to an assertion that art can live a daily life, and that art has a role in our daily lives. The fusion of art and daily life quickly became a tenet of the early twentieth-century avant-garde, but it was also a concrete goal, and one that had a political impetus. Once daily life was executed along artistic principles, many early avant-gardists felt, the general populace would be released from the lethargy of dead-end materialism, and culture could no longer be used as a simplistic index of class distinction and/or an avenue of political manipulation.

The quotidian and the political are inherently connected, but while the daily has stayed in the foreground of European and North American poetics, politics has not always been as prominent. For several reasons—not the least of which is the atmosphere of global political crisis that has so far dominated the twenty-first century—poets are again putting the two together, but searching out ways to do it differently, to do it obliquely, using the arts to refine and enlarge the definition of the political.

For Peter Gizzi, the political starts with the word itself, and he keeps it connected to its root in the polis. His individual poems are often set there, in the city, which he sees both as a dense heterogeneity and as community, but he also makes the poems themselves into cities—they are diverse but synchronized collectivities. The long poem "Etudes, Evidence, or a Working Definition of the Sun Gear," from *Some Values of Landscape and Weather*,[1] operates as a city in this sense, but it also brings us to a real city, Marseille, to examine human confluence and its potential for community. Stylistically, the poem is representative of much of his work in that it blends three tendencies from three historic periods: a twentieth-century fascination with the daily, manifest in both language and content; a late twentieth-/early twenty-first-century aesthetic of fragmentation that implicitly explores the distinction between juxtaposition and disjunction; and an early nineteenth-century Romantic appreciation of loss.

Gizzi's engagement with the daily parallels those aspects of American society that are increasingly secular and committed to the immanent as opposed to the transcendent, trends that date back to the early nineteenth century. In his work, however, the daily is more immediately rooted in American Modernism from Pound and Stein through Williams and on up to the New York School, whose writers had an eye for the poetic within the everyday to the highest degree. Gizzi's poems are full of objects we see all the time—freeways, flagpoles, birds, bricks, and clouds. His poems evoke familiar situations that take place in recognizable surroundings, and he presents them in speech-based phrasing: "How come all the best images are uncanny?";[2] "Spider webs are scarier / when you have a mortal disease, / or just creepier, more final / somehow."[3] His language leans so heavily on the daily that it pushes into the realm of the vernacular; choices such as "How come," "scarier," and "creepier" are not only mundane, they're aggressively casual. They belong to the ephemeral world of passing conversation, which fights with the permanence of the printed page on the one hand, and creates a ghostly echo in our ear on the other.

Ephemerality is the temporal version of the fragment. Gizzi's ghostly echo, like all echoes, manifests in shards, in fleeting audio glimpses. The ephemerality of daily language gives the echo a swiftness that makes whatever it brings us zoom by, caught only in the corner of our ear, which suggests that the postmodern fascination with fragmentation is in part a fascination with motion. In Gizzi's work, that motion is usually double—whether heard or seen, both the thing perceived and the perceiving thing are moving, which requires a sort of perceptual calculus, for which poetry, with its tendency to keep language itself in motion, is uniquely suited.

Gizzi's work fragments both in form and in content. His normally correct syntax breaks down rarely enough to keep its ruptures startling, yet often enough to establish syntactic fragmentation as a deliberate aesthetic and philosophic choice. Aesthetically, it accentuates edges and, like the high-contrast shots of film noir, contributes a honed, attentive, almost nervy feel that counterpoints the complacency that his often homey imagery and phrasing might otherwise invite. Philosophically, fragmentation opens up abysses that implicitly question the balance of absence and presence—is what is *not there* more powerful in its absence and insinuation than what *is* there? Fragmentation tests our intuitive notion that there's a hollow at the core of things—is it a hollow? Or is it a bit of antimatter to match every bit of matter? Irresolvable, the fragment is demanding. It forces the reader either to "tread water in mid-air" or to finish, at a split-second's notice, the unfinished impulse of another. Any fragment questions the very concept of completeness, just as it questions the concept of the incomplete, asserting the validity of all those anarchical things that cannot be made into parts of some larger whole. Any fragment allows the essentially heterogeneous nature of the world to show through, and in this way, Gizzi's poems are realistic.

His fragmentation also highlights a play between juxtaposition and disjunction. Though these two appear similar, they imply radically different approaches to and assumptions about connection. They both startle, and they both split the mind's attention, a little like a stereoscope fitted out with two different images, but while juxtaposition makes us aware of the immense potential for connection across physical and conceptual abysses, disjunction raises the possibility of irreconcilable difference. Taken together, they make us consider their very distinction and query our own sense of the world's integration. Is this a world with sufficient inherent connectivity to allow almost any two things to shed some kind of light on each other, as juxtaposition argues, or is it one that features a "center that will not hold," generating perspectives that can't be reconciled? Each view has its political ramifications, and while neither is "true," there may be a truth revealed by the alternative one chooses. For the most part, Gizzi chooses juxtaposition, which is another version of the reconciliation of opposites so important to the Romantics.

In many ways, Gizzi's work is firmly rooted in the Romantic tradition—his are, for the most part, first-person lyric poems focused on the emotions as experienced by an integrated and consistent subject, with love as the ruling sentiment. That love often takes the form of longing, which by extension becomes a love of longing itself. And a longing *for* the self—a nostalgic glance backward by an "I" that can't quite believe in the ideal, consolidated subject to which its very existence pretends and the coherent world that such a subjectivity constructs, even as it speaks from that subject position. "I want an art that can say how I'm feeling," he states in "Revival"[4]—in a tone and context shot through with the unattainability of the "I" as well as of the art. A line further down in the poem, "For want of a sound to call my own," is equally ambiguous—is it the "sound" or is it the "I" behind the "my" that's missing? Or both? And to what degree are these losses interdependent, with the "I" disappearing for want of a vehicle of expression? The slightly tongue-in-cheek opening of another poem, "A History of the Lyric"[5] ("I lost you to the inky noise"), shows that he's aware of his investment in loss, and aware that it's bound up with writing, thus with representation, thus with doubling. It's a loss we're all refusing to let go of in this society increasingly invested in representation.

On the other hand, throughout Gizzi's work, there are lines and passages that adopt the Romantic posture without apology or other subtext. "Desire rose in the lofty tree of those evenings,"[6] states one, with the single word "those" making the evenings impossibly distant, as inimitable as the originals are unattainable. Gizzi uses loss/longing to establish something analogous to atmospheric perspective—a series of receding tones that draw the reading mind further on. This allows him to go beyond the Modernist immanence-of-the-daily without encountering the problems of hierarchy imposed by transcendence. He also uses loss to record and explore a very real, acute sensation, one that's both personal and political. The entire long poem "Revival" is about the loss America has made of itself, and about the dangerous way that we compensate ourselves for that loss by enjoying it. It's the principle that drives an Edward Hopper painting, and we keep updating it everywhere from popular songs and Hollywood movies to the "retro" craze in home decorating.

These three stylistic principles—focus on the daily, fragmentation, and longing—come together in the theme of "Etudes, Evidence,"[7] which is signaled by its epigraphs: "Many elements are common to many things, as letters are to words" (Lucretius), and "The organization of movement is the organization of its elements, or its intervals, into phrases" (Dziga Vertov). In the broadest sense, the question that both haunts and drives Gizzi's poetry is "How are things put together?" Which quickly extends to "And how do they hold?" "Etudes, Evidence" adds another layer to these questions by asking how deep the structural parallel between language and the physical world goes. Is there any accuracy—and/or is there any point—to asserting that the elements of the world are arranged according to a kind of syntax? And what kind of order does that syntax demand? Is it a restrictive one or a generative one?

Early on in the poem, Gizzi establishes a parallel, not only between language and the physical world, but specifically between language and the city, and he does it through simple splicing, using the same kind of juxtaposition that characterizes the urban landscape. The phrases "full, volumetric night, scribbling streets," "the color blue today has 26 hues," and "the shaped light is making the curve of an *s,* / loop of *e,* the crown of *a* as boats / in spilled ink sway . . ."[8] all occur on the first page. This is an urban walking poem, in the family of Apollinaire's "Zone," in which to walk is to inscribe the body into the landscape, but, appropriately for the twenty-first century, he has added a virtual dimension to the physical—though the poem travels the city, it does so, in part, from a window, underscoring the mind and the imagination as modes of travel. In both its virtual and its actual aspects, the journey is a true one in that the "I" emerges changed, but at the same time, because it's an urban journey, it's circular; it leads nowhere. There is no distance covered, only ground. This is also true of another, much shorter poem in the book, "It Was Raining in Delft."[9] The way that the "I" walks that city, recording impressions and his speakers' reflections on them, suggests a causal relationship—the things of this world cause the things of the mind. It's a subtle demonstration of Williams's "no ideas but in things."

The world, then, walks into the person, rather than the other way around. This view of the human/world interface is particularly apparent in a cityscape, which, unlike a landscape, has no horizon to pull one along a progressive, linear path; instead, it constantly mirrors itself, as well as one's own face, in buildings and windows; its roads keep turning corners; urban public transportation runs in circles, and more and more, cities are bounded by ring-roads, more effective barriers than ancient city walls.

These poems model an intensive rather than an extensive kind of walking, which has a correlative in poetic rather than discursive uses of language, in that both intensive walking and poetic language work by building up layers on a predefined and limited surface, compressing and complicating it. The sun in the title "Etudes, Evidence, or a Working Definition of the Sun Gear" is emblematic of this for Gizzi, who has commented that the Mediterranean sun feels so intense and so ancient that it resembles a *nihonto,* a Japanese sword made by pounding the metal out and folding it back upon itself time and again. "Etudes, Evidence" is a poem of arrivals; it operates as a gate, taking in whatever comes, and taking it as it comes, letting it impress itself upon the otherwise blank page. In a graphic echo of Spicer's radio model, it is taking the city's dictation.

Gizzi's work is inflected not only by Spicer's notion of the radio, but also by his concepts of tradition and atemporality. On a sheerly material level, atemporality is inherent to poetry because, though rhythm may be language's timekeeper, it is syntax that makes that time unidirectional, and even poetry such as Gizzi's that uses the full sentence often takes syntactic liberties that disrupt time's itinerary and contribute to a general temporal suspension. And atemporality is entwined with tradition. Only through the denial of time enacted in the *writing to* inherent in, and only in, poetry can a poet of today converse with poets of earlier eras—with the Troubadours, with the singers of the *cante jondo,* or with any poet from the past—without having to reduce that poet to the terms of the present. As Spicer contended, such atemporality is, in fact, contemporaneity, for contemporaneity has nothing to do with time—one's contemporaries might be centuries in either direction. Rather, it's based on a slippage of ideas, which is itself made possible by alignment—again, a spatial rather than a temporal issue, a matter of making two spaces so contingent that they become shared—the space of the poem.

Among other things, the city, both as metaphor and as lived experience, becomes a way of mapping this space and of tracing the path of the body within it—"if nerves map a city," Gizzi suggests in "Chateau If," and then goes on: "if a city on fire / if I say myself am I saying myself."[10] The poem is not about a city, but about the intersection of the self and its art *as* a city, which is the "city that overtakes the city I write."[11]

The one common denominator among all Gizzi's projects—writing, translating, teaching, and editing—is their focus on community. And his poetry alone forms a body of work that makes readers and listeners consider what community means. Perhaps at its most basic, it simply means "us," an equally slippery, but less abstract term, for while the referent may slide, it's always composed of tangible bodies. And in asking about "us," we must also ask about "them," for any mention of an us automatically supposes a them—an other in some kind of, if not opposition, at least contradistinction to us. And yet Gizzi, curiously enough, has almost no "them" in his poetry; instead, it's full of "I," "you," "we," and "us," which amounts to a radical assumption of responsibility and a refusal to see anyone as categorically other. And it's consistent with his attempts to build community through a query of and eventual retrenchment of the self. For the most part, he uses the terms "you," "we," and "us" in both an intimate and an open-ended, inclusive way. Anyone is welcome to step into the "we" of a line such as "The difficulty of being here is what do we transmit of ourselves that we can ever really know?"[12] Gizzi's pronouns not only welcome everyone; they assume, even require, everyone's participation.

Reading Gizzi's work makes you a member of a community. And though it's true that all acts of reading create community, because Gizzi is particularly focused on this role of literature, access to community through his work is unusually heightened.

You enter his pages and become a word among other words—"you" or "we" or "us," or even, through empathy, "I." And thus, Gizzi's poetry constructs a community of words, a city of words. But it's not the famous city of words that Plato discusses in the *Republic*—that just city that exists only in the mind or soul; it's a city of words that can and does exist on earth, and that can, through its dedication to the polis, have a political effect in the world.

NOTES

1. Peter Gizzi, *Some Values of Landscape and Weather* (Middletown: Wesleyan University Press, 2003).
2. Ibid., 49.
3. Ibid., 44.
4. Ibid., 47.
5. Ibid., 11.
6. Ibid., 31.
7. Ibid., 69.
8. Ibid., 69.
9. Ibid., 81.
10. Ibid., 82.
11. Ibid., 83.
12. Ibid., 33.

News That Stays News

Documentary poetry has had an increasing role in American letters throughout the twentieth and into the twenty-first centuries, and it offers an opportunity to look at American society's assumptions about the relationship of language to truth. Central to such work is the problem of how to reconcile the language of information with the language of art. William Carlos Williams in "Asphodel, That Greeny Flower" raised the possibility for this reconciliation: "my heart rouses / thinking to bring you news / of something // that concerns you / and concerns many men."[1] He also acknowledged its difficulties in the same poem: "It is difficult / to get the news from poems / yet men die miserably every day / for lack / of what is found there."[2]

It's difficult to get the news *from* poems because it's difficult to get the news *into* poems. What role does poetic language, or poeticity itself, play in that difficulty? Though perhaps the first question we need to ask is what, exactly, is news? To start with, it's information with a particular relationship to truth and to time. What documentary work does, in part, is to put pressure on those relationships, exposing our assumptions about the connection between truth and transparency, or ready accessibility, as well as between truth and origin, urgency, and poeticity.

We can begin to explore poetry's relationship to truth by contrasting it with that of fiction, whose nontrue nature is central and both achieved and announced by the fact that it imitates the true through presenting facts, entities, actions, situations, etc. that mimic those in the outside world. The distance from the actual world offered by mimicry and imitation is what allows fiction the perspective to comment upon that world. However, the alternative worlds that poetry sets up, to the degree that it does, aren't miniature copies of the world at large;

instead, they operate by other logics, according to other laws, and at other speeds. And for much poetry, there is no "outside world"; rather, it constructs a new element in the world we all share, and as an actual element of that world, it cannot *not* be true. In short, it cannot make truth claims because it is itself a true act.

For instance, just a few lines picked almost at random—these are from Paul Hoover's poem "Childhood and Its Double":[3]

> *Everything's more real, once it finds its mirror.*
> *The gray lake and its gray sky,*
>
> *Skin and the sound of drums,*
> *And the back end of a costume horse*
>
> *Confused against the skyline.*

The opening line—*Everything's more real, once it finds its mirror*—indicates, through its syntax, that it participates in the truth-economy of the world-at-large, that it is making a positive assertion, but in fact it doesn't; the logic it obeys operates only within its own boundaries (the poem), within which the statement is true, but once taken outside those boundaries, where it must function on other terms, it would quickly be called nonsense (which in its own way is also always "true"), for, though stating things about objects in the real world, the line does not attempt to replicate or represent that world in an accountable way. The images in the lines that follow cannot be held to the truth test either because they declare only themselves, their own existence, and make no claims beyond that.

So fiction and poetry are both, in their own ways, absolved from the truth test, whereas, documentary—no matter what its genre—cannot be: its whole purpose is to present as accurately as possible events in the outside world, and its value is based on the degree of that accuracy, which means that documentary poetry has a paradox at its core, a clash between two, contradictory relationships to truth.

Documentary work is based not only on presenting a truth, but often on unmasking a lie or an either intentional or accidental misconception or misrepresentation, and documentary poetry is no different, often addressing situations that the general public doesn't want to face for any number of reasons from guilt by complicity to its own open wounds. Thus, much documentary poetry—or any documentary—starts out facing denial and doubt, which lands it with a burden of proof, or at the very least, the job of witness. This in turn raises complex issues of voice: Who is speaking for whom, and what is the basis of one's right to speak for another? Who has the right to speak of a given event or situation? Only the people directly involved? This view might be inferred from one of the seminal examples of documentary poetry, Charles Reznikoff's books *Testimony* and *Holocaust*, in which he uses only the words of participants. Yet these words were taken from testimony given in formal courtroom situations, so while every word may be that of a participant, the "voice" itself has been changed, first conditioned by the conventions of the courtroom and then sculpted by Reznikoff's process of selection and arrangement. Such treatment/transformation illustrates the fact that it's impossible for one person to present another's voice unaltered; this issue haunts any documentary project, as avoiding appropriating the experience or voice of another often requires repressing one of the writer's principal tools, the imagination.

A shift away from imagination and toward what is in this case its opposite—the truth—presents a shift in what we usually think poetry can and should do, revealing that it can be an effective part of civic life and can bring the news in a way that no other form can. If poetry can do this, its ability to do so must be bound up with poeticity (defined here as the poetic function in Jakobson's sense—putting the focus on the message for its own sake—along with figurative language, image, ambiguity, and juxtaposition). This amounts to bringing language as art into the heart of the language of information. This tension alone accomplishes something by positing an incommensurability at the center of the work, an irritant that demands attention and refuses complacency.

Mark Nowak's work offers an opportunity to look at these issues in action, particularly his 2009 book, *Coal Mountain Elementary*, and his 2004 book, *Shut Up Shut Down*. Both books focus the reader's attention on situations that American society can all too easily ignore because those who don't live in or visit the affected areas never see the results. Each book's project is, in part, simply to bring the reader to this other world, a world determined by industrial disaster and decay. *Coal Mountain Elementary,* which deals with mining accidents in China and the United States, is, like Reznikoff's work, constructed entirely of the voices of others, which in a certain way means it's exclusively using the language of information. These voices speak in coherent, prosaic paragraphs, so one might ask in what way this is poetry, and what framing it as poetry gains for the project. The first question is less interesting; whether or not it's poetry is a moot point, but the fact that declaring language normally considered prose to be poetry *does* accomplish something *is* interesting. It underscores the impossibility of unmediated language; it emphasizes context through the roles of editing and positioning, and it heightens contrast. Throughout the book, Nowak splices together three different bodies of information so that the alterations in tone make each one more particular, more resonant, as the work builds. There is no default tone that can settle into a background hum and become routine; the reader is constantly alerted to the particularity of voice and detail.

Though not the most important, part of what makes this poetry is its use of the visual: the visual aspect of language is always poetic because it obstructs transparency. As soon as we are seeing language, we are no longer seeing through it. Here the visual is asserted by the way the text is cut and positioned on the page, which creates a dynamic exchange with the considerable stretches of white space, and controls the pace at which information travels through silence. Nowak also uses contrasting roman bold, roman text, italic, and colored typefaces to create a back-and-forth dynamic through accounts that are both crucial and tragically repetitive. But the largest visual element is the numerous photographs, which ironically literally bring language back into the picture, as many of the photographs are of signs, so while we're reminded of the cliché "a picture is worth a thousand words," how do the numbers work out if the picture is *of* words?

Many of the issues that drive *Coal Mountain Elementary* are also at work in Nowak's earlier text *Shut Up Shut Down,* which documents the effects of unemployment caused by factory, mine, and plant closures. It also uses three different typefaces and uses extensively, though not exclusively, the voices of others, many extracted from newspaper accounts, which means that the same voices, the same statements, have been refracted through the very different lenses of newspaper and poetry. One of their principal differences is time: a newspaper account comes at the end of something, the end of the event reported. It is urgent; its purpose is to inform you of something that *has happened,* to "get the news out"—and why there's a universal assumption that *we need to know everything as quickly as possible* I don't know; after all, the event has occurred, and there's nothing we can do about it now. So a newspaper article tends to seal the issue shut. Documentary poetry reverses the process: its account comes at the beginning of something, and its purpose is to inform you of something that *should happen.* It does not accept the closure effected by the newspaper, does not accept that "there's nothing we can do about it now." By refracting the same material through a different lens, a completely different demand is made. The language on the page is not only trying to convey this; it is also trying to incite it, which makes it no longer sheerly descriptive language, but pushes it into the performative, making it an action with the potential for real effect in the world. And that real effect will be another action, this time on the part of the reader. Language that causes action is itself action.

In Nowak's work, this language is strongly marked: it's stripped bare; it's aggressively clear: few adjectives, few adverbs, lots of concrete nouns and familiar verbs, and little or no figurative language, rhetorical or structural play, or ambiguity—all characteristics that amount to a low degree of poeticity. These are the characteristics that are central to the appearance of truth and the economics of trust in our culture. It is precisely where urgency is greatest, where the need to trust the truth of the text is greatest, that we see the lowest incidence of poeticity. The stripped-down, nonfigurative, nonsuggestive, nonassociative language attempts absolute transparency, a 1:1 relationship between sign and referent, because the writer knows that that is more likely to be believed.

And he's right—in the United States today, the general belief (though unexamined and usually unconscious) is that truth comes only through direct, nonfigurative, unornamented language. This is bad enough, but even worse, the inverse is also true: the average American-on-the-street expects to find lies in ornamented and figurative language. The tiny percentage of the population that thinks about poetry, or even language, theoretically (or at all) might say, "No, no, we expect to find nontruth in ornamental, figurative language," meaning the nontruths of non sequitur and nonsense touched upon earlier, but the general public, without realizing it, actually expects to find lies, which means that we have an active bias against poetic language in our culture. In other words, the flip side to poetry's not being liable to the truth test is that it is assumed to be incapable of conveying truth. We saw this bias in action during the 2004 presidential election, when John Kerry was vaguely but generally mistrusted by a large number of Americans because they didn't "understand" (instantly and unambiguously grasp the paraphrasable meaning of) his eloquent speech because of its complex syntax, rhetorical sculpting, heightened vocabulary, and figurative language. The unspoken but very clear statement was "If I don't understand it, it's a lie," a conviction that creates a conflation of understanding and truth that allows for the even more dangerous inverse assumption that "If I understand it, it's true."

Given this bias on the part of the general public, why present documentary work in poetic form? Because poetry—amid all its ambiguity and ornamentation—is not only perfectly capable of conveying truth; it can also attain a unique relationship to truth because it implicitly acknowledges and interrogates the limitations of language. The truth of a human situation can't fit into language (contrary to the tacit assumption of journalism) because human truth surpasses fact. However, through interstices opened up by figurative language, ambiguity, juxtaposition, sound relationships, and rhythmic patterns, room can be made for those aspects of truth that can't be articulated. Work such as Nowak's starts with the truth-as-clarity equation, but through subtle introductions of poeticity, it introduces a broader sense of truth that recognizes that the fully complex version must incite the imagination of the reader, must get the reader beyond simply absorbing facts and into a responsive engagement with them because that engagement is a crucial part of truth. It's the emotional part, which can't be told; it must be felt, which can be achieved through imagination, but not through idea. What makes Nowak's work extremely effective is that he knows how to do this subtly.

In *Shut Up Shut Down*, for instance, he incorporates poeticity in a number of ways and at a number of levels, through the sculpting of the text blocks on the page, through the play of overt sound relationships and varying tones, and through ambiguity and implication working alongside testimony and declaration, but all of these are employed in such delicate doses that many readers will not be aware of them, per se.

The first series in the book, "$00 / Line / Steel / Train," uses the form of the haibun, a Japanese form based on the incommensurability of poetry and prose—and on the assumption that incommensurability can, if stretched to the point of aesthetic effect, have a social and political effect as well. It's also a form traditionally engaged with travel; haibuns are travel accounts out of which certain moments are distilled into suspended sparks of insight, which is bitterly ironic here, as Nowak's text is about people who are going nowhere, both literally and figuratively. At the same time, however, the haibun form dignifies their experiences as aspects of the human journey. In this case, the moments of insight are not smooth epiphanies, but routinely fractured, splintered glimpses. And the prose paragraphs of the "journey" against which they are figured are multivocal, making voice itself into the journeying element, traveling from one mouth and one story to the next.

Visuals have an important place in this book too, even when they don't show up. This first series is numbered after Bernd and Hilla Becher's photographic series *Industrial Facades*,[4] though the images themselves are not included, and yet they're rendered more powerful by their absence, as it underscores the absent faces that should be framing the voices we hear on the page. Another series in the book, "June 19, 1982," puts text in direct dialogue with image, again photographs (with all their problematic assumptions of veracity) and again facades—with all their disturbing insistence upon the face, facelessness, facing it. The dialogue between photo and text is rhythmic and determinate, with the photo on the left-hand page, which underscores the photos' muteness, as this is the silent page: when a book is open to the full spread, there is a cultural bias toward the right side, or recto page—in part because most people are right-eyed as well as right-handed, and in part because it's the first side exposed when the page is turned; whereas, the left side, or verso, is the one that's left blank to indicate a new section or chapter, and in some books, it's routinely left blank. The fact that these photographs are always on the verso reinforces the sense of "silenced faces" that is introduced by the brutal degeneration depicted in the photos, and serves as yet another reminder that truth cannot be contained in words.

This series also employs heightened sound relationships, particularly rhyme, which make a stark contrast to the flat, declarative sentences that precede each lineated section, seeming to reshuffle the information and re-present it at a different pace. The change in pace makes the reader incorporate it differently, complicating the receptive habits that equate clarity with ease of assimilation, and making the careful reader aware that the transparency that seems to guarantee truth also encourages passive acceptance.

Throughout, the distinctly poetic elements take care not to announce themselves too loudly for fear of compromising the text's credibility. Other recent documentary poetry projects take a similar approach to poeticity, using it subtly, deftly, to open language up enough to allow it to exceed itself without going as far as the ornamentation that raises suspicions.

Claudia Rankine's 2004 book *Don't Let Me Be Lonely*[5] focuses not on a world out of sight to most of us, but on the repressed in the everyday, particularly that related to class, race, and above all death, accumulating into an altered perspective on classism and racism based upon our society-wide refusal to acknowledge death. The documentary frame, established by the neutral tone as well as by the inclusion of fact-based, "objective" information, often gleaned from the news, doesn't demand that we acknowledge a masked world as much as it returns us to our usual surroundings with a critical eye. However, there's a curious twist at its core in that, with its pervasive and autobiographical "I," it's also documenting a subjectivity, thus complicating documentary's implicit claim to objectivity: can there be such a thing as an objective account of subjectivity? This posture points the work in two directions—on the one hand, it's aiming for public inclusion in both content and address; it's the very fabric of the public itself that she's talking about, and on the other hand, it's an inquiry into private space. One of the book's projects is to find the point at which these two can construct each other responsibly.

Thus tension rules the work, a tension echoed by the claim, on the book's cover, of its being "an American lyric," while its tone and content deny that categorization. What is the purpose of underscoring this as poetry? And is that what "an American lyric" would be anyway? It's a useful tension in that it keeps the book from ever settling down; instead, it's constantly gently tearing itself apart from inside and out.

As in much documentary work, Rankine uses a flat, direct voice that seems to be working patiently and constantly to earn its credibility, to establish its sincerity, which, as in Nowak's work, is based on the warrant that a text is believable, is sincere, is *true* exactly to the degree that it is clear. There appears to be an almost complete suppression of the poetic function (which in many minds is essential to lyricism), and little figurative language. In particular, there is no metaphor or simile, a tacit recognition that "nothing is like anything else," which is crucial to the claims she's making. On the other hand, she makes strong, subtle use of pun (the main character is a medical writer writing about "the liver"), juxtaposition, non sequitur, and threading (elements or details that reach back to other places— not long enough or close enough to be considered repetitions—but small details that echo and haunt and set up a system of overtones). All these elements relate to connection and its problems. By restricting the poetic to these issues, she places the issue of connection at the center of the work, and indeed, the negative results of the apparent inability of Americans to make proper connections is her main point. But because her poetics is doing it for her, she is spared the didactic.

And that, in turn, allows her to remain speculative, which is to say, internal. She can continue to appear to speak to and of herself alone, which avoids all risk of appropriation. The text incorporates a considerable amount of reported speech, but reporting another's speech is very different from speaking *for* someone else. She controls all the voices in the text by keeping the "I" as the constant lens. Thus we believe the veracity of the claims made to the degree that we believe the "I," which in turn is based on the degree that we believe *in* the "I."

And most people find her "I" convincing, and yet it turns out that, in fact, it's not true. The things recounted did not actually happen to a single person; a lot of what the "I" tells us did actually happen, but to someone else. How does that affect both the truth of these statements and our belief in them? For most people, it seems not to make much difference; they still believe in the "I" because they believe in the book's principal claims about social justice—and they believe them because, in fact, they haven't been counting upon this "I" to fulfill the documentary imperative of informing us; we already have the information from other sources; we know that these statements, if they aren't themselves true, are at least representative of the truth, and this we know from our own observations—her "I" has simply made us aware of this, as well as of the deeply human and personal dimension; it has reminded us that the news is a personal thing. Yet this isn't the nontruth of fiction because it doesn't set up the parallel but imagined world. Its world remains fragmentary and testamentary, with the "I" finally revealing itself to be the eye of society, a communal point of view whose multiplicity and complicity the book makes us confront. Part of the disarming quality of Rankine's text is her awareness of all of this and her overt grappling with it: "If I am present in a subject position, what responsibility do I have to the content, to the truth value, of the words themselves?"[6] Ultimately, it is the sincerity of her attempt to grapple with it all that we "believe."

Photographs also play a role in Rankine's text, though unlike Nowak's "June 19" images, these aren't silent. They do something quite different, which is to point to an overflow of information, a world in which everything is speaking at us. Her most recurrent image is of a television screen, but there are also many images of language-as-disembodied-directive: labels from medicine bottles, post office circulars, messages written on a slate. This constitutes a type of speech to which one cannot respond. It is in effect speech whose sole goal is to silence its seers.

Brenda Coultas's "Bowery Project," from her 2003 collection

A *Handmade Museum,* also deals with the repressed in public space in an attempt to make us aware of and accountable to certain aspects of daily urban life that are tempting to ignore. And though it also uses transparent language with a carefully restricted degree of poeticity, the entire project functions as a metaphor. Ostensibly a catalogue of trash and its recuperation through dumpster diving in the Bowery, the text also creates an undeniable echo of the way we treat the homeless. She keeps this from getting heavy-handed by incorporating humor and by maintaining a predominately factual tone, so in this case, "fact" not only equals trustworthiness; it also offers a way to avoid the pitfalls of moralizing and blame. "I found X on X day," she says. By giving the date and location of many of her encounters, fixing them in real time and space, she increases the sense of veracity, and thus, by implication, accountability. These markers are part of a general self-consciousness that adds another level of transparency to the text, one that lets her step outside its frame and declare her intentions in statements such as, "In order to transform into a public character, I need to claim a public space. I will sit in a chair in the Bowery at the same place and time for a season and participate in and expedite street life. I'm going to dump it all in, everything that occurs to me or everything I see. That will be my data, my eyes upon the street; the firsthand observation of this last bum-claimed space."[7] The phrase "dump it all in" reverberates with the overflowing dumpsters that landscape the text, and offers another occasion to question our definition of trash. Her humor is mostly ironic and is the mechanism by which that irony is accepted. The irony here is that of the abundance of poverty, poverty that is spilling out of garbage cans, streaming along the street, an unrestrained flood of the useless, the broken, the empty—a world drowning in its own lack.

Poeticity plays a larger role in this text than in the others, for while it seems to be as transparent as possible, both frank and intimate at the same time, it's also highly metaphoric. Not only is the overarching metaphor mentioned above reinforced on every page by images of people carting piles of garbage around, trying to resuscitate it, trying to reclaim its value, but the text also includes many specific metaphors and similes; for instance, in describing a growing pile of discarded bottles, she writes, "the glass was rising to the top of the chain links like a transparent pool without swimmers."[8] She also uses rhetorical structures, such as anaphora, parallelism, and litany, but despite these ornamentations, overall, this text too has a relatively low degree of poeticity.

As exemplified by these three writers, the focus of much documentary work remains on the subject matter, with an implicit call to action. Language is at the service of information, and yet they have devised ways to make the language of information even more informative by subtly augmenting it with the language of art. However, there are other instances of documentary work that are doing what might seem to be almost the opposite. Language in such cases is more at the service of art, and its writers have devised ways of making the language of art even more aesthetically complex by augmenting it with the language of information. This shift is based on a shift in urgency. Such texts are not calls to action, but calls to reflection. Rather than wanting to get us out into the world doing things, they want us to reconsider, to think more deeply, and they use poeticity to slow down our assimilation of language, to encourage us to take detours, to ponder alternatives. Such texts are often no less socially oriented, but they operate in a different time frame.

Susan Howe is a strong example of a writer working in this vein. Over the past few decades she has woven together ongoing research in a number of subjects, many involved with New England history, from captivity narratives, to early religious sects and their leaders, to Dickinson, Melville, Peirce, and Stevens. Accumulating from book to book, these interests get more deeply intertwined until the reader of her entire oeuvre brings several layers of fact to each line or section. The facts lead toward the poem, rather than issuing from it. And in consequence of (or to facilitate) this change of direction, we see a much greater degree of poeticity.

At times, as in her 1997 book, *Pierce-Arrow*, Howe documents the act of research: "During the summer of 1997, I spent many hours in New Haven in the bowels of Sterling Library."[9] This framing accomplishes many things, and one is to establish the voice of veracity as a frame for the book, implicitly promising that any factual material that appears is, in fact, reliable. But it also allows her to wallow in the notion of and possibilities of research itself—she is, in these passages, researching the impulse to research, and through that, the role of documentation in the constitution of knowledge, which is then, in the poem series that follow, contrasted with the role of invention in the same pursuit.

But these documentary passages detailing her working methods quickly turn out to be not-so-documentary after all, as sentences written ostensibly in the language of information turn out as unsuited to stand the truth test as most poetry. Descriptive lines such as "The microform room at Sterling has several new microfilm readers with Xerox copiers attached"[10] give way to lines in similarly but deceptively normative syntax, such as "It is strange how the dead appear in dreams where another space provides our living space as well" or "Documents resemble people talking in sleep."[11] As mentioned earlier, these statements cannot be said to be true or false because they aren't participating in the economy of truth, even though they use its vocabulary and syntax. Howe approaches these issues head on: "I can spread historical information, words and words we can never touch hovering around subconscious life where enunciation is born, in distinction from what it enunciates when nothing rests in air when what is knowledge?"[12] She embarks on a vertiginous balance between rigorous inquiry and the recognition that normative language necessarily reduces truly new thinking—that normative language, by its very normativity, cannot accommodate the act of thinking; it can only accommodate thought, its prepackaged past tense.

Oscillating between such considerations of the role and limits of knowledge and the facts of Peirce's biography, Howe maintains a dynamic surface that also tells a story sufficiently to establish the basis of what is to follow: a dissolve into a completely different kind of language in which poeticity rules and the visual qualities of language are maximized. Though this may seem opposite to what Nowak, Rankine, Coultas, and other such writers are doing, in fact, at its core, it is driven by the same concern for the news, for while the primary goal of Howe's research may be to create a base for her poetry, the goal of that poetry is, in turn, to constitute an alternative mode of knowledge, a mode in which truth has nothing to do with clarity, but rather with novelty. It's a different kind of news in which only the unprecedented is true.

NOTES

1. William Carlos Williams, *Asphodel, That Greeny Flower and Other Love Poems* (New York: New Directions, 1994), 18.

2. Ibid, 19.

3. Paul Hoover, *Poems in Spanish* (Richmond, CA: Omnidawn Publishing, 2005).

4. Bernd Becher and Hilla Becher, *Industrial Facades* (Cambridge: MIT Press, 1995).

5. Claudia Rankine, *Don't Let Me Be Lonely* (Minneapolis: Graywolf Press, 2004).

6. Ibid., 54.

7. Brenda Coultas, *Handmade Museum* (Minneapolis: Coffee House Press, 2003), 15.

8. Ibid, 27.

9. Susan Howe, *Pierce-Arrow* (New York: New Directions Press, 1997), 5.

10. Ibid., 5.

11. Ibid., 6.

12. Ibid., 6.

News That Stays News

GENERATIVE BRIDGES

To Writewithize

(as in "to hybridize," "to harmonize (or ritualize)," "to ionize," etc.)

I write entirely with my eyes.

—Gertrude Stein

For most of the people ever likely to read this essay, poetry is primarily a visual experience. Even the most avid attenders of poetry readings probably encounter much more poetry through the eye than they do through the ear. One of the implications of this shift toward the visual is an increased emphasis on the visual aspects of language, which in turn requires that we change the way we talk about verbal/visual relationships. We need to make distinctions between different types, for different types of relationships create different products on both ends—or, differently stated, the nature of a relationship determines the natures of the two things being related, and poetry and visual art are both changing in response to their new interactions.

The engagement of the visual arts by poetry is traditionally known as ekphrasis. The OED's definition of the word is enormously vague, but the way the word is currently used is more precise. In its broadest sense, it is understood as "writing on art," and a perusal of various common dictionaries delivers definitions such as "the painting of pictures with language," "the matching of words to images," "translating a visual representation into a verbal one," and similar. In practice, the term indicates the product of a writer's consideration of a painting, sculpture, Grecian urn, Achillean shield, or other specific work of art. It implies a mirroring action, carefully positioned and constructed, and can be, because of that, revealing, almost reflective, of both poem/poet and art/artist.

But it can also be limiting; the traditional ekphrastic stance accentuates the separation between the writer and the object of art. The writer remains not only mentally outside the visual piece, but often physically in opposition to it, literally standing across from it, in a kind of face-off, in a gallery or museum. And often the physical stance echoes the emotional: despite the apparent homage, there's frequently an element of opposition, a tinge of rivalry and/or challenge inherent in this mirroring—can the poem match the painting in impact? And/or be a "faithful" translation of it? And there's a tinge of protection—writing is used to keep art at a safe distance, to keep it sealed in its frame, demonstrably the "other" of poetry. This is not to deny the sincere homage in such works, nor to speak too slightingly of this relationship—merely to pose it as but one mode of ekphrasis in order to consider some others that take the term in different directions.

One mode that holds closest to the contemporary use of the term, and yet actually acts very differently, includes works that don't *look at* art so much as *live with* it. The principal difference here is not in the verb, but in the preposition. A side-by-side, a walking-along-*with*, replaces the face-to-face relationship—the two, poem and artwork, are presumed to be going in the same direction and at the same speed; they are fellow travelers sharing a context. Some examples include Carol Snow's *Artist and Model*,[1] in which issues of framing, perspective, and resemblance filter throughout the book, and art is just one more, albeit crucial, element of the everyday world. The implied viewer shifts constantly; at times it's the "I," which sometimes looks and sometimes is looked at, framed in a window or otherwise arranged as a composition. At other times, the viewer is the work of art or is dispersed throughout the world. There is no single, sovereign position. Specific artists are evoked, but are not the subject of the poems in either sense; rather the artists participate in the poems, sometimes with bits of conversation, sometimes with their own obsessive imagery. The result is a version of the daily in which art is normal—not special, not something removed from the quotidian flow and isolated in a frame or institution, but an inseparable part of the daily—and the poetic—weave.

Though extremely different in tone and style, Laura Moriarty's *Nude Memoir*[2] also engages *with,* grapples *with,* visual art, particularly Duchamp's *Given.* The book is not about the work; rather, it lives with the work and its disturbances, and it uses *Given* to negotiate those disturbances as they appear on myriad levels, which is, arguably, what the piece itself is attempting to do, which means that *Nude Memoir* is not only not opposing or competing with *Given,* but collaborating with it. In order to do this, Moriarty must, among other things, erode the boundary between *Given* and other works, such as Hitchcock's *Vertigo* and the poet's own life. The relentless folding over of images maintains this confluence of "real lives" and "works of art." Throughout, the book implies that frames—whether in a movie or around paintings—are compartmentalizing gestures used to construct a sense of comfort and control, as well as containers to keep art carefully separate, functioning as commentary on life, rather than as an integral part of it. By breaking down such frames, Moriarty makes art both vehicle and substance of an odd truce between daily life and its troublesome undercurrents.

Mei-mei Berssenbrugge's *Sphericity*[3] breaks down the division between art and daily living even further. There are no specific works mentioned and no frames to break open. Berssenbrugge is not erasing the line between art and life; it simply isn't there. But all the elements of both are—color, line, surface, form, and motion. And so are all the questions that traditionally animate a work of art; distance, interpretation, perspective, illusion are here applied ambiguously to life and art both, so that the reader is constantly aware of the presence of the visual arts without being able to delimit them, for, finally, there is no outside to the work, no division between art and body and world. This seamlessness is underscored by her calm, rolling rhythms and contemplative repetitions.

In these examples, the operative relationship is not so much between a writer and a work of art as it is between verbal and visual modes of experience, both of which the writer lives. All three examples expand upon traditional ekphrasis by deviating from it at the referential level, which is its habitual realm; instead of using visual art as subject matter, works such as these increasingly use it as a model for formal construction, thus underscoring the arts as modes of thinking and perceiving, rather than as static objects.

Another way the traditional ekphrastic approach has been broken open is by incorporating the visual in a variety of literal ways, such as through a heightened attention to page arrangement and page space. This approach, which has precursors in George Herbert's and other Renaissance shape poems, and more recently in the Modernist experiments of Mallarmé's *Un coup de dés* and Apollinaire's *Calligrammes,* reaches an extreme that transforms it into its own genre in the work of Augusto and Haroldo de Campos and the many other practitioners of concrete poetry. It shifts the ekphrastic focus from "writing on art" to "writing as art" and requires a new conception of figure-ground relations in which white space becomes an additional signifying element. Though his primary interest in the page was as a dynamic score for breath and voice, Olson further opened it up with his emphasis on field, and in the past fifty years, the resulting manipulations of page arrangement, presenting it as a visual space in its own right, have offered such an important direction for experimentation that it's now a feature that immediately distinguishes much late twentieth- and early twenty-first-century poetry from its predecessors, and has established a new basis for further experimentation.

Johanna Drucker's work is an extreme example of this direction and, more directly than most, engages and challenges the traditional boundaries of ekphrasis. Her books *The History of the/my Wor(l)d*[4] and *The Word Made Flesh*[5] enact a verbal-as-visual event on every page, while her books *A Century of Artists' Books*[6] and *Figuring the Word*[7] theorize and document the history of this fusion, and related developments, in detail. All of these are published by Granary Books in New York, perhaps the best source in the country for this kind of work. Its catalogue *When Will the Book Be Done?*[8] not only presents the books it's published, but also gives full-color proof of the variety and wealth of late twentieth-century visual/verbal intersections, not just on the page, but also in three dimensions, through questioning the form of the book. Granary Books' publication *Poetry Plastique,*[9] the catalogue of an exhibition that also explored this expansion into the third dimension, held at the Marianne Boesky Gallery in New York in 2001 and curated by Charles Bernstein and Jay Sanders, presents a particularly helpful historical sweep. The works included were, in Bernstein's words, "not poems about pictures, but pictures that are poems."[10] Word and image neither translate nor illustrate each other, but work inseparably as single compositions. And in this case, the compositions were hung on gallery walls, taking ekphrasis off the page and giving it a much larger territory.

Though particularly pronounced in the *Poetry Plastique* work, in all cases of such close interaction, word and image are working at "right angles." They're conceptually perpendicular to each other, and thereby set up a conceptual three-dimensionality, which is to say that the mental and the physical worlds are not perfectly congruent; we find ourselves undergoing two different interpretive practices simultaneously, and their degree of off-set sets up a reverberation. Energy arcs over that gap, almost palpable. And it requires an adaptation if not of our senses, at least of our perceptive capacity. Viewed in this way, it's not we who are working on art, but art that is working on us.

NOTES

1. Carol Snow, *Artist and Model* (Boston: Atlantic Monthly Press, 1990).

2. Laura Moriarty, *Nude Memoire* (San Francisco: KRUPSKAYA, 2000).

3. Mei-Mei Berssenbrugge, *Sphericity* (Berkeley: Kelsey Street Press, 1993).

4. Johanna Drucker, *The History of the/my Wor(l)d* (New York: Granary Books, 1995).

5. Johanna Drucker, *The Word Made Flesh* (New York: Granary Books, 1996).

6. Johanna Drucker, *The Century of Artists' Books* (New York: Granary Books, 2004).

7. Johanna Drucker, *Figuring the Word* (New York: Granary Books, 1998).

8. Steven Clay, *When Will the Book Be Done?* (New York: Granary Books, 2001).

9. Jay Sanders and Charles Bernstein, *Poetry Plastique* (New York: Granary Books, 2001).

10. Ibid., 7.

How Ekphrasis Makes Art

Much of twentieth-century art was about the relationship between object and viewer, and one of its great lessons involved the power of looking, its potential as a creative process in its own right, and its part in constituting the art it sees. To paraphrase Wittgenstein, all seeing is seeing as. This idea is perhaps most readily available to contemporary sensibility through Duchamp's readymades, which have become almost a cliché of the mundane object transformed into art by being viewed as such. As soon as that happens, different aspects and details of the mundane object seem to leap out, and different questions and assumptions are applied to it.

Despite the hopes of the early avant-gardes to fuse art and daily life, the gaze that transforms an object into art does so in part precisely by removing it from daily life, and it's the very things that ruin a bicycle wheel functionally that make it able to function aesthetically, namely isolating it from bicycle and road, and making its motion arbitrary, useless. As all art does, the readymades flaunted uselessness in celebration of the abundance that such indulgence in the useless implies.

Though it seems the two were unaware of each other at the time, Duchamp in his readymades was working from the same principle that the Russian Formalist Viktor Shklovsky outlined in his work on *ostranenie,* or making strange.[1] Both relied on a radical alteration of context to make an object bizarre or uncanny, which in turn allowed the viewer or reader to see or experience it in all its particularity, as if for the first time. By extension, we don't actually see (literally or figuratively) an object per se; what we see are concerts of objects in dynamic interaction. As Shklovsky emphasized, changing an object's field of interaction, its context, changes the object itself, which is further transformed, determined, and delimited by the angle and set of assumptions from which we view it.

Traditionally, ekphrasitc poetry establishes a direct, often one-to-one relationship with a work of art, which means that its object has already been judged to be a work of art, and usually has been labeled as such by an entity or institution—a museum, a gallery, a critic, etc. The ekphrastic poem therefore reinforces the institutional judgment (as well as reinforcing a notion of poetry as an *other* to art, rather than an art itself). But there's a different sort of ekphrastic poetry emerging in the work of some contemporary poets, an ekphrasis that, instead of looking at acknowledged artworks, constitutes the gaze that transforms an object into art. This ekphrastic gaze changes the object's context, aestheticizing it, which is not to say that it beautifies it, or makes its inherent beauty apparent, or renders it in some way pleasing; it is to say that it shows it in new relationships, revealing internal relationships among parts and their relationships to other things. Poetry's ability to speak literally, figuratively, abstractly, and concretely all simultaneously enables it to analyze the intricacies and interconnections of a given thing while also keeping its holistic and nonanalyzable nature to the fore. This altered emphasis on relationship—or emphasis that alters relationships, making them strange—is in part achieved by delimiting and situating; such ekphrastic work makes art by framing its subject and altering its perspective.

These gestures are readily apparent in some of Stephen Ratcliffe's work, such as his 2002 book *Portraits and Repetition*.[2] Many of the poems in the book were written at the rate of one a day, sitting at the same window at the same hour of the morning. That routine is in itself a frame, artificially and intentionally cutting an instance from its surroundings in both space and time, but there is often a more concrete frame as well, and often it's as immediate as the window itself, with the perspective established by his position at this window. The act of writing from this position becomes an act of selection, isolation, compression, and arrangement, aestheticizing the scene by composing its elements in a way that makes each element both itself and a counter, a foil working with and determined by the other elements in the scene. It is this doubling of function—making elements both themselves and counters, making them both immanent and transcendent—that makes the scene into a work of art. For instance, this couplet, which begins one of the poems:

7.9

how (it) takes place in the space between leaves and the air
it touches moving it, darker foliage behind such an event[3]

In these lines, we see a precise act of framing taking place; discrete sections are neatly cut out of the world as a whole, sections in which there are a limited number of elements, which allows us to see their interrelations clearly, which is one of the principal services performed by a frame, be it cinematic, photographic, pictorial, or literary. Ratcliffe's sequences in this book are all written in couplets, which is, in itself, a framing device that takes the space of the page left blank and turns it into a functional element.

There is never an "I" in Ratcliffe's work, so, just as the viewing person never actually sees her- or himself, in these poems, we the readers are immersed in the imaginative body of the viewer; we become that body, becoming that point of view, and in so doing, become the act that transforms the land before our mental eye into a landscape. The couplet above, in addition to becoming a landscape, also raises philosophical conundrums—what is the "space between leaves and the air"? And what is *it* that touches? It is unnameable, inextractable, and therefore retains an undiluted power. A little later in the same poem, this couplet:

white door opening to absence of horizon the bird disappears
into for instance, which (*is*) also what a man first hears[4]

Ratcliffe's doorway neatly, classically, experientially, frames a scene that evokes, rather than includes, a horizon and a bird. Just as a landscape painter will choose a section of the world and distill within it selected objects, the gaze of the writer is choosing and, through that choice, distilling the scene into just a few of its elements, thereby emphasizing their relationships. Thus they become not only themselves and counters, but also the terminals of relationships, which always slightly transform them: the relationship between the bird and the horizon, for instance, or between the bird and the doorway, becomes as important as the bird and the doorway themselves and alters them.

While this work is similar to what a landscape painter does to transform land into landscape, painters are limited to the sense of sight, whereas writers, because they engage no one sense exclusively, but rather have access to them all through the additional quasi-sense of the imagination, find themselves much less limited. For instance, here, in response to the phrase "which (*is*) also what a man first hears," the reading mind opens the hearing sense and starts looking for connections. Grammatically, what is heard is the "for instance," but since that doesn't intuitively sit quite right, the mind retains it, but continues on, trying out "bird" (yes, that could be audible), but the bird isn't actually there, so on we go to the white door opening, in other words, to the frame itself, until, in the mind's ear, we're hearing them all: the frame, the framed, and that which has escaped the frame—and, above all, we literally hear the sound frame of the "disappears/hears" rhymed couplet. Poetry can capture all of these; painting can't—it can get the frame and the framed, but what escapes the frame escapes painting as well. So, here poetry is making what it looks at into visual art, and then is dimensionally surpassing the art medium that it most strongly evokes. And yet in other instances, poetry is brought up against its own limitations and particularities.

9.11

vertical edge of window against which light (describe) hits, grey-white expanse of ridge filling in space to the right[5]

In this couplet, the word "describe" stands in for the fact that it cannot be described—by using the imperative to instigate a distance rooted in timelessness, Ratcliffe effectively eternally defers the obligation to describe, while simultaneously making us aware that we really don't need the description: there are some words, such as "light," that are their own description. It is stated, and thus it is, and this is one of those rare instances in which this is-ness is sufficient.

The issue of sufficiency, just like the issue of excess, is always present where there is a question of aesthetics, for aesthetics is always concerned with achieving presence, and recognizes that it is the *arrangement* of the present that makes presence possible—not in the sense of re-creating a scene or event so well that you feel like you're there, but by creating a new, entirely separate event right where you actually are—to make being in the poem an experience as strong as having been in the scene the poem evokes—and that ability to be in the poem can only be achieved by a proper balance of elements within the poem itself. Ratcliffe's poems are composed of such subtle selections, distillations, framings, and analyses of internal relations:

7.6

(*how*) color looks in different light, red roofs of buildings
to the left of which chimney against the neighbor's house

bodies in room watching images on wall (*it*) appears to echo,
something she feels coming toward this line at that angle

man on ladder for (example) sanding by hand, shape continued
moving forward and back in relation to the ridge above it

white between planes of glass through which the green leaves
(*completely*) still, as if events hadn't started to happen

before the woman in the car calls, man being loved by others
as the physical manifestation of an idea itself, (*more*) so[6]

Ratcliffe's tone is always precise, always careful; he leads our eye with almost painstaking patience from one object or situation to the next, always letting the single noun, its enormous presence, evoke rather than describe, and it is precisely this slowness that allows each noun to grow to such a size—to such a size that it looks strange—just strange enough to make us look twice, and see the thing rather than its name.

John Taggart approaches the question of the aesthetic quite differently from Ratcliffe, but in some of his work, he makes the same gesture of transforming land into landscape, which is to say, into a work of art, particularly in "Pastorelles," the title series of his 2004 book *Pastorelles*.

Large round bales at random
on the field
which looks shaven looks pool-table smooth

trees in the woods
around the field the sky above seem bigger more absolute
the field an absolute field a form framed by an arching
      border of trees

because of the large round bales

Stonehenge-like/free-standing/strange

when the bales are now departed in their rickety and red
      wagons

everything =
the familiar = the invisible
for which one weeps if one weeps in sheer gratitude.[7]

In many of his poems, Taggart makes the sudden move toward emotion at the very end, which works because we have
been led through the scene so carefully that we're absorbed in
it and have arrived at that emotion ourselves. Here, he leads us
by turning the scene into a painting: starting with the dominant
forms, the hay bales, he moves our eye, as the shapes in a painting might, to the field on which they're standing, then to the
trees in the background and the sky above, and finally to the
fact that it's all "framed by an arching border of trees." He then
deftly moves from that painting to another dominated by the
startling and vivid image of the laden, rickety, red wagons, in-
voking a series that traverses time in a single image.

Taggart also engages the notion of *ostranenie* fairly directly:
"the large round bales // Stonehenge-like/free-standing/
strange." The analogy with Stonehenge makes a leap through
time, space, and culture to start us off seeing them anew, and the
word "strange" finishes reorienting our point of view.

The final twist that comprises the end of the poem is based
on this notion as well: the familiar = the invisible, yes, but here
he goes somewhere a little unexpected, to the deep, deep gratitude of being able to take such things for granted, gratitude for

the fact that such a pastoral peace is indeed, here at least, granted. Of course, the very fact of the poem belies this casual attitude: Taggart is clearly seeing what's around him in all its life and dynamics.

The poem "Pastorelle 5" complicates the ekphrastic stance by opening with the more traditionally ekphrastic gesture of looking at an acknowledged work of art:

Pastorelle 5

There is a poem scroll
early Edo period 17th century
plum trees branches painted in gold
blossoms of the plum tree painted in silver

black squiggles
over some of the blossoms

and there is this

snowfall
around midnight
two of all the sycamore's leaves remaining
two gigantic shadows out over the road around midnight
tattered and gigantic
upon the new fallen snow.[8]

The line "and there is this" divides the first half of the poem from the second and is isolated in its own stanza, which has the effect—because it comes before its antecedent—of making *this* be just exactly *this*—not the thing he's about to describe, but the instant of presence itself, our attendance on the present moment, which is an enactment of the state to which the view to be described conveyed him.

Then we get to the scene, and the roughly parallel structures of the two halves of the poem (six lines apiece) suggest that if the Edo scroll is considered a work of art, then this must be considered one as well, and by extension, then, the very poem we're reading is the poem written in the margins of the scene before the writer's eye that makes it, too, a poem scroll.

Ekphrasis that makes an object or scene out in the world into a work of art allows the reader to be present at the precise moment that art is made, at the instant of the shift from presence to representation, when something slips from the perils of time into the distilled space in which it can come to mean more than itself. It can be argued that when something comes to mean more than itself, it has thereby lost itself, but as the passage of time is inescapable, this mode of seeming to save the moments, things, and scenes we value is better than losing them altogether.

NOTES

1. Viktor Shklovsky, "Art as Technique," in *Russian Formalist Criticism: Four Essays,* ed. Lee T. Lemon and Marion J. Reiss (Lincoln: University of Nebraska Press, 1965), 3–24.

2. Stephen Ratcliffe, *Portraits and Repetitions* (Sausalito: Post-Apollo Press, 2002).

3. Ibid., 151.

4. Ibid., 151.

5. Ibid., 215.

6. Ibid., 148.

7. John Taggart, *Pastorelles* (Chicago: Flood Editions, 2004), 75.

8. Ibid., 39.

A Hand Writing

The word "line" presents a world of ambiguity: is it the "line" of verse, with its specific metrical or syllabic structure, or perhaps something written quickly, as in "I'll drop you a line," or is it, on the other hand, a line drawn as all or part of a visual image? Though often unnoticed, there's a point where these two converge, a slippery instance at which writing actually becomes visual art and visual art becomes language. And though it manifests in writing/drawing, it impinges equally upon seeing/reading, raising the question of whether or not reading is a specialized form of seeing, one achieved, ironically, only by sublimating seeing in the normal sense, for when we read, we need to look right through the material aspects of the word in order to access referential meaning more immediately. Other modes of seeing, such as viewing visual art, emphasize the opposite. In learning to view visual art, we are trained to remain attentive to that very materiality.

What, then, happens in the brain when we view art that demands both reading and seeing? And why did the instances of such art increase dramatically throughout the twentieth century? In his book *Inner Vision*,[1] the neurologist Semir Zeki argues that art is purposeful, that it has developed to train the brain, to sharpen its abilities to better meet the tasks of daily living. And, obviously, as our environment changes, so must our brains. In the past fifty years, we've seen more and more work, by writers and visual artists both, that incorporates language in ways that constitute a visual element and a linguistic one simultaneously. Do we read such things, or do we see them? And does art that rides this line between reading and seeing cause the brain to perform two tasks simultaneously that it would normally perform separately? And does this, in turn, prepare our brains to more effectively deal with the changes in technology, as well as the speed and insistence of visual stimuli (advertising, television, video games, flashing signs, etc.), that have become increasingly prevalent in the past several decades?

As children grow into adults, they get encultured into a reading that denies or sublimates the seeing, thus narrowing the written object to only one of its aspects. The aspect that we privilege is the more complex, in that it requires additional levels of interpretation and more highly trained engagement to render it meaningful. In other words, it takes more training to learn to read than to learn to see, and that fact alone elevates it on the scale of prestige and contributes to its precedence to the point that most literate adults read without seeing what they're reading. This dichotomy can also be considered as one between product and process: reading has a clear, definable, and transferable goal; it has exchange-value in that after a text has been consumed, it can be exchanged as "marketable" information or added to a store of enabling knowledge. Seeing, on the other hand, is an end in itself, consuming no object and resulting in nothing that can be passed on.

The purpose in making this distinction is not to argue their relative values, but rather to explore the possibility of dissolving their dichotomy and striking a balance between—or opening up the field between—reading and seeing to create a different zone of perception. Handwriting, as opposed to printing, offers an approach to this, as it allows us to both read and see at the same time.

Imagine a continuum of perception whose extremes are pure reading—looking right through the marks to their meaning—and pure seeing—regarding the marks with an attention that remains within them, not translating them into something else. Throughout recent art, there are extremely charged works that fall very close to the middle, suggesting a growing delight with playing with this line. Particularly striking examples include Henri Michaux's "faux" ideograms, drawings that he executed with varying relationships to written language. If you do an Internet image search using the key words "Henri Michaux Narration," you'll find one from 1927 influenced by his recent travels in China and Japan and his fascination with the radically different way that ideograms construct their meanings. Using the key words "Henri Michaux Movements" will get you to a very different work from 1951 that has an even more ideogrammatic feel, while also suggesting the human form, creating a compelling fusion between body and writing, the body as writing. Some of his drawings, such as many published in the Drawing Center's *Untitled Passages*,[2] go on to suggest writing as migration, with the progression of an illegible text seeming to merge with a long line of travelers on a horizon. Michaux's work is central to thinking on asemic writing—writing that has no specific or determined semantic content. Christian Dotremont's logograms, which you can see by using those as key words for an Internet image search, offer another excellent example; here the graphics do actually present words, but they have been so stylized as to become "illegible," intentionally fusing semantic and visual content. Contemporary practitioners of asemic writing include the Dutch artist Serge Onnen, the Australian artist Tim Gaze, and the United States artist Michael Jacobson, who also runs the blog "The New Post-Literate," which features asemic writings.

Just on the other side of the increasingly compromised line between the written and the drawn is writing whose graphic presence tends to make us discount its content and focus on its nature as design. Adolph Wolfli's background-writing, many beautiful examples of which can be seen by image-searching his name, dissolves to sheer, rhythmic pattern to form the ground against which other aspects of his compositions figure. These backgrounds imply not only language, but specifically handwritten language, as the white noise of contemporary civilization. Another excellent example of such work is Robert Smithson's well-known "Heap of Language" (again, just do a search with his name and the title), in which we see handwritten language as a mountainous, monumental form, a dominant feature of our cultural landscape. The fact that it is handwritten foregrounds the gestural, asserting language as an act not just of the mind, but also of the body. There are many other examples I could cite, and all draw attention to a zone of "between-ness," a highly psychologically active zone that puts more and more pressure on the constructed distinction between the written line and the drawn line, implicitly proposing other constructions.

Such works may also be teaching us things about ambiguity that keep us able to deal with the ways that ambiguity is changing in contemporary society. For instance, the increasing prevalence of type over handwriting masks language's inherent ambiguity. Type tells us that language is clear, uniform, and instantly decipherable, while handwriting functions as a visible metaphor and powerful reminder that language is never monosemantic, but always multivalent.

2

We can also look at this another way, using another continuum, one that focuses on ambiguity itself. The extremes of this second continuum would be the Lindisfarne Gospels or the Book of Kells (images of which can be found by doing Internet searches for those titles) and black letter gothic (also easily accessed through an Internet search), on one end, and on the other, a Cy Twombly canvas such as *The Wilder Shores of Love* or many others in which the viewer must become immersed in the writing in order to decipher it. Both extremes accentuate the role of time in the construction of meaning, while the center point, occupied by any number of san-serif typefaces, attempts to mask that dimension completely.

The continuum, laid out as such, might look like this:

```
informal. . . . . . . . . .uniform/neutral. . . . . .formal
Cy Twombly. . . . . . . . . . .Futura . . . . . . . . . .Book of Kells
```

This continuum has a middle point opposite to the other's; here instead of a complete fusion of drawn and written line, we have a kind of zero-degree of letter form that aims for complete transparency and the least ambiguity possible. Futura, which is the typeface you're reading now, offers a good example. It is the skeleton of the letter with all ornamentation removed. It's almost invisible, and its goal is to be invisible. If you move out from its essentiality in either direction, while legibility does not become impaired until you get toward the extremes, ambiguity starts creeping in from the very first deviation. Every added serif, every added curve, adds to the eye's entanglement in the letter as image. Consider, for instance, Times New Roman, then *Alexei Copperplate,* then ℬℰℰℋℐVℰ. The letterforms in the series get progressively more difficult to decipher, which slows down their translation into meaning and complicates the meaning they do achieve. As soon as you get into handwriting, the ambiguity is dramatically increased because you not only have adornments to the skeleton, you have irregular adornments, for the very nature of handwriting is to be unique at every stroke, and it always carries subtle information about the writer's personality and state of mind. This information can't be articulated precisely or consciously tracked, but it contributes to the content of the handwritten message.

Handwriting itself has been getting a lot of attention in the past few decades, by everything from its frequent appearance in works of visual art to facsimile editions, such as that of Duchamp's *Notes,*[3] or popular books such as the Griffin and Sabine series.[4] Handwriting has become the focus of scholarly investigation, and such studies often look not only at a manuscript for the development of thought as revealed by corrections, eliminations, and additions, but also at the writing itself for its intrinsic aesthetic qualities. This approach was the focus of the headline exhibition at the Bibliotheque nationale de France in the summer of 2001 on "the brouillon"—the rough draft, the work in manuscript.

All show an interest in reevaluating the rough draft—it has become beautiful, and not just as a preparatory step to a "finished" printed product, but as a finished work in its own right— or rather, as an unfinished one, as its attraction lies precisely in the fact that it isn't finished, that it can't be finished, which means it never ends, but remains alive, growing in the mind of the reader. The contemporary attraction of the unfinished goes beyond the art world and into popular culture—we see it everywhere from raw edges on chic clothes to distressed furniture— the one not-yet-finished and the other a finish that has come undone. That which is coming undone has an inherent beauty that the finished lacks because it acknowledges time as a partner to all creative endeavor, while the not-yet-finished, in its rawness, retains the momentum of its creation, just as handwriting seems to retain the momentum of its inscription as a latent energy. Or perhaps contemporary culture finds these states of imperfection attractive because they show us where they fail and seem unafraid to do so. The paradox of vulnerability displayed unflinchingly is a banner advertising inner resources that few of us can match.

Handwriting, in flaunting this rawness in much recent art, accomplishes several things:

It constitutes a site of the confluence or conflict between the claims of the social and the claims of the individual. Handwriting, being necessarily unique, registers a resistance to being absorbed by or into the social, and thereby always runs a check, maintains a balance, between these inner and outer, public and private, realms.

At the same time, it is the link, the conduit that makes of the body and the world a single system. It is an avenue through which the body extends itself out into the world, literally inscribing itself upon it.

Handwriting is rhythmic in a way that type can't be; the rhythm of type is necessarily even, whereas handwriting can incorporate all sorts of variations, which allows it to keep the beat of language, which is the beat of thought, impression, response. It records the body marking the beat of the world, thereby underscoring that the world has a beat.

Related to this is the inherent dynamic of the handwritten line, and the equilibrium struck by that dynamic. Through its ascenders and descenders, its loops and circles, the written line is a constant struggle for—and a threat to fall beyond—equilibrium. Thus it's a medium under constant tension, resolved at the horizontal axis, which operates as a zero zone, a hum. There's something in the drama—and it is a drama—that is played out in miniature, symbolized, that is deeply humanly appealing. It is the human drama of emotional push and pull, of rising and falling fortunes; it's an elaborated electrocardiogram that yet remains generic—it's all of ours—that a handwritten line records.

Handwriting is language lined with a second, parallel language, the unpronounceable, wholly phatic language of human presence. If writing always attests to the absence of the writer, handwriting retains a vestige of the body to warm that absence.

Related to this, words always include other words—their sounds recall other words, and their visual appearance always incites flickers of others—for instance, the word "world" always flickers right on the edge of "word," "work," and "would." These are ghosts within the word, and in the handwritten word, with its lower legibility and higher ambiguity, these ghosts remain especially active.

Handwriting subverts and compromises the authority implied by printed text, an authority that is based on its invisible source. Printing, lacking all trace not only of emotion, but of the entire human being, seems to speak from the sky. Handwriting, on the other hand, divulges its origins; it's not only human, but a specific and vulnerable human that yet still retains the power to speak, to state. Handwriting is an implicit insistence on the right and ability of the individual to speak out.

A word never has the same meaning twice because it is always in a different context. We think of that context as sheerly linguistic—the other words around it—but context also includes the appearance of the words, their typeface or handwriting and the surface they're written or printed on. We would readily agree that in spoken language tone and inflection dramatically affect meaning; similarly, the way in which a word is written alters its meaning; its physical qualities are contextual contributions, and handwriting records these in a way print cannot.

And though words are always altered by the various chains of other signifiers they slip into and through, destabilizing them, the signification achieved by the physical attributes of those words—color, quality of line, density, etc.—is more stable precisely because they are even more ambiguous than the words themselves. A word, because of its relative specificity, suggests immediately other things it could be, other directions it could be going. Those directions are largely traceable; no sooner is a word posited than it's off and running. But color, line, etc., are much more open-ended, so while they're active, they're "running in place"; they don't go anywhere, which is to say they don't go anywhere except deeper into themselves. This quality of going deeper into themselves rather than out along an associative chain is crucial—it means that compositions that employ these two kinds of signification have an extra internal and internalizing dimension, and that their words are "stopped" at least momentarily in their own flight along the signifying chain.

Handwriting is a site of the eruption of the semiotic. The disruption, instead of emerging within the referential aspect of language (and disrupting it), emerges within the physical, heightening and emphasizing the signifying potential of the physical. This puts the semiotic and the symbolic in an unusual relationship—a kind of simultaneity that offers more augmentation than disruption.

Handwriting is a landscape, which is to say that it contains more distance than its surface can literally account for.

Consider these two relational triangles:

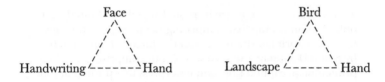

Face is to bird as handwriting is to landscape as hand is to hand. Hands are the vestiges of man's attempt to create a new language, a language of distance made intimate—and handwriting is the trace of that new language even as it bows to convey the words of the old one.

NOTES

1. Semir Zeki, *Inner Vision* (Oxford: Oxford University Press, 1999).

2. Henri Michaux et al., *Untitled Passages* (New York: Drawing Center, 2000).

3. Marcel Duchamp, *Notes,* ed. Pierre Matisse (Paris: Centre Georges Pompidou, 1980).

4. Nick Bantock, *Griffin and Sabine* (San Francisco: Chronicle Books, 1991).

The Fold

As phrased in a 2004 auction catalogue, where it was listed start-ing at eighty thousand pounds, the object under discussion is:

> Cendrars, B. *La prose du Transsibérien, et de La petite Jehanne de France.* Couleurs simultanées de Mme. Delaunay-Terk. Paris. Editions des Hommes Nouveaux. 1913

> 4 sheets, 50 × 35 cm. each, pasted together. Printed recto only, 2 columns, the first comprising the letterpress title, justi-fication, imprint at the head, and the huge coloured pochoir by Sonia Delaunay: the second column comprising a colour-printed map, caption-title, and letterpress text printed in four colours, the margins and indentations filled with watercolour. Folded within the original parchment wrapper, with hand-coloured pochoir design by Sonia Delaunay.

La prose du Transsibérien, et de la petite Jehanne de France was the first simultaneous book. You can easily find an image of it by using the title as the key words of an Internet search. Published in the "annus mirabilis" of the Modernist era, it was a collabo-ration between the visual artist Sonia Delaunay-Terk and the poet Blaise Cendrars, who owned and ran the house, "Hommes Nouveaux," that published it. It was announced as an edition of 150, and its publicity claimed it was as tall as the Eiffel Tower—at two meters each, the 150 laid end to end would have matched the tower's three-hundred-meter height.

In a world in which the *livre d'artiste* itself was new, their book made yet another new gesture. The *livre d'artiste* emerged at the very end of the nineteenth/very beginning of the twentieth cen-turies, when a few people interested in fine-press, often gallery owners such as Ambroise Vollard and August Kanwheiler, commissioned and then produced elegant limited editions of poetry or fiction by contemporary writers in collaboration with works by contemporary visual artists. Now-famous pairings include Bonnard and Verlaine, Picasso and Jacob, and Apollinaire and Derain. They were revolutionary in that they focused on living, relatively unknown writers and visual artists and gave equal space to text and to image; however, they accentuated the independent worlds of the verbal and the visual by keeping word and image strictly separate, often giving each its own page—image on the verso, text on the recto, for instance. The *Transsibérien* exploded this rigid division, using a number of moves to fuse text and image, and in so doing, created a third, hybrid object that was neither verbal nor visual, but an intricate interfolding of the two.

Delaunay-Terk repeatedly stressed that the visual component was not an illustration of the text; she claimed in an interview with André Salmon that "the simultaneity of this book is in its simultaneous and non-illustrative presentation. The simultaneous contrasts of the colors and the text form depths and motions that come from a new sort of inspiration."

In Delaunay-Terk's and Cendrars's *La prose du Transsibérien*, structure determines nature and is its most innovative aspect. Composed of multiple folds, it foregrounds the mechanical. All books have moving parts, and therefore have a mechanical aspect, but by putting the motion where it's not expected (by distributing it all across the surface, instead of concentrating it in the spine), by putting it out there in full view, and by making it the exclusive structural element, they underscored mechanics in a way that aligned their work with numerous contemporary experiments in the aesthetics of the machine, from the Eiffel Tower to Marinetti's manifestos to Duchamp's nude.

At the same time, the *Transsibérien* contributed to what was at the time a widespread, though in this case contradictory impulse to return to roots or to a more "primitive" state, prevalent in the work of the Russian Futurists and some Cubists, for the artists chose the oldest book structure known, the scroll. However, having begun with that bow to the origins of the book, they quickly moved on, updating it with aspects of that quintessentially modern genre, the advertising poster. By blending the ancient form of the scroll with the latest artistic movements and color studies, they presented the entire history of the book—simultaneously, and yet marked with the scars, the creases, of those intervening centuries, marks made by their modernization of the scroll itself. For theirs is a scroll that refuses to *roll*—again the innovation focuses around motion. In a way, what they created is a Cubist scroll, a geometrical clash between the most basic elements, circle and square. By folding instead of rolling, they squared the circle, transforming its continuity into a series of stops, of stations toward an end that does not come back around, which is echoed in the poem's content. In its final refusal to return lies its final modernity.

The refusal to circle back around can also be read as a refusal of closure, which is given a positive spin by the fold: one folio doesn't need to close in order for the next to be opened. There are no severed edges, but we still get the pacing of pages and the distinction of discrete units, yet they are units that remain always in sight of each other, and always in sight of the larger project of which they are a part; in short, we get all the pages simultaneously, yet they remain separate pages. These pages remain even when the work is hung because use has made the folds fundamentally different from the rest; the folds stand out; they are stains.

They called it "the first simultaneous book," but what makes it a book and not a poster? The fact that it's read not for information but for aesthetic power, that it's not useful or occasional, that it can't be consumed in a glance. That it can't be consumed—it can only be used, despite the fact that it's not useful. Which suggests that if we can use information, for instance, that in an advertisement—if the language allows us to attend the event or purchase the product—then the language has been consumed; it has been incorporated and transformed, fundamentally changed in nature; if it doesn't allow that, then we must use it in an intransitive sense, which is to say we use *it*, but the *it* doesn't become something else, *it* doesn't conform to the imperative of transformation inherent in the commercial transaction. We must use it, but to no purpose. The *Transsibérien* not only raises this problem, but leaves us in the middle of it. And the middle is huge. When unfolded, it's of inhuman size; it can't be held or really even handled, which violates one of the hall-marks of the book: its intimate relation to the human body. De-launay-Terk and Cendrars emphasized this by underscoring the relationship of the entire edition of 150 to the Eiffel Tower. This placed the book beyond the body and brought it into the realm of the monument.

There are other implications in this insistence: the single "object in question" is in fact not whole in that it takes the en-tire run of 150 to be complete. This adds a new dimension not only to this, but to all books. What you hold in your hand is but a fragment. Delaunay-Terk's hand-painted visuals heighten this because each fragment, each copy, is unique, and so is precisely *not* a copy and cannot be replaced by any other. The real book is the connective tissue, the concept that runs between and links all these finished fragments.

The between, another version of the middle, is a fertile space that's been much theorized in the past few decades, but it was also a crucial element of Modernist thinking, and the *Transsi-bérien* epitomizes it, for the fold is, above all, a between. And yet, unlike most betweens, it's more solid than the two things it con-nects. It thickens, and every act of folding and unfolding thick-ens it further. This isn't conceptual, but physical; it's simply the nature of paper: repeated articulation separates the fibers, lets them expand. The between begins to cast a shadow.

The whole project of the *Transsibérien,* not just its product, is a between. Its inception and production lie in conversations between two people, while the actual object lies between the vis-ible and the legible, between the spatial and the linear, between abstraction and representation. The text supports this; it de-scribes a journey strung out between Moscow and the sea, and then between Russia and Paris. Conceptually, aesthetically, and physically, the *Transsibérien* is a fold between zones whose in-tegrities are never compromised by their coming together.

A fold is a coming together. A fold is always intimate; it de-mands and it offers intimacy. And of the deepest sort—intimacy with itself. The other may be hard to face, but facing the self allows no escape. We're constantly folding books shut. I know of only one poet, Claude Royet-Journoud, who plans the space of his pages to insure that the lines of the recto interlock precisely with those of the verso when the book is shut. This is an intensive understanding of the fold. Delaunay-Terk and Cendrars practiced an *extensive* understanding: what happens when the fold goes on and on, when it becomes an extension of space.

The *Transsibérien* was folded once vertically and then twenty-one times horizontally to fit into its parchment wrappers. The twenty-one folds are accordion, and this act of folding back on itself has implications. The very phrase "accordion fold" emphasizes music, and is a way of making the music inherent in the poetry, and the musical imperative of poetry, a physical, structural element. The book has become musical instrument. That's just a pun, of course, and there's always something superficial in a pun, but it's precisely that superficiality that makes it appropriate to the *Transsibérien*. So much in the *Transsibérien* keeps us on the surface, from the vivid color to the nonfigurative language. It's a text that insists on surface, and its folded structure both emphasizes and enriches that, for the layers inherent in an accordion fold multiply the surfaces, create a seriality of surfaces that amounts to an elaborate refusal of depth. And yet, a fold also creates an interior on the surface, a functioning contradiction that complicates dimensionality—it's more than two dimensions, but less than three. The fold confuses the outside/inside distinction; it reveals each as contingent, and always apt to find itself the other.

This foundation in paradox has other manifestations, for to fold back (as the accordion requires) is to cancel out while also adding. Switchbacks up a steep mountain: you retrace your steps, but not quite; the return doesn't quite undo the going, but you haven't progressed very much either. It's an act of place-holding in which the place gets augmented. Energy builds up—much expended, but not extended, creating an energetic singularity, a rhythm that crosses neither space nor time. (Again, simultaneity.)

Accordion folding is a rocking—a physical rhythm at the base of the book, which in this case echoes the rocking back and forth between text and image that the piece, unfolded, encourages. So we unfold to another kind of fold, that of our own perceptions bringing left and right columns together in a kind of *mille-feuille* of shifting attention, constantly folding one side into the other, an enfolding that gradually erases the abyss that runs its length, the one left by the initial physical fold.

To fold is to encrypt a line, to increase its density and to imprint it with itself. A cryptogram. A crypt. A fold always hides something, and often creates what it hides by the act of hiding it. It's a constructive obfuscation, creating at the precise point of absence. The accordion fold is a special case of this, as it allows for different aspects to be hidden or visible at different times; it creates a constantly changing configuration of fields, a dynamic of presence and absence. But it's one in which the absence is always more actual, for though, as claimed above, physically the fold is constantly expanding, conceptually it has no substance. It is activity that occurs nonmaterially, and in that way it is metaphysical.

All moving parts are composed of two or more nonmoving parts articulated, except where the fold comes in. A fold can make a moving part of a single thing. Thus the fold is articulation itself. Put another way, the fold is the basis of difference, establishes difference, inaugurates difference; it can make two of one without occasioning any qualitative change. It can create difference out of and all across any surface. This is one of the definitions of traveling: creating difference out of and all across a surface through motion. The fold is inseparable from travel—it is raw motion. It moves the nonmoving thing. It takes an extension and makes it go. It's pure travel in that it's the going without the having gone. There's no territory covered. Given the content of the poem and both Cendrars's and Delaunay-Terk's peripatetic backgrounds, this traveling distilled to book structure is particularly fitting.

The description of the *Transsibérien* coming up for auction mentioned at the beginning ends with this note: "Because of its folded presentation, this work is usually damaged or torn in the gutters of these folds." The fold is the site of vulnerability because the fold is the site of transfer, the crack in the surface, a rent in the fabric that lets the world leak in, and that acknowledges the intrusion of the world as a vital element in art.

Translating Writing/Writing Translation

People who both translate and write are often asked about the relationship between the two—in the abstract, but also in the particular, in terms of how translating influences the practice of writing; however, the very question may be misleading in that it implies if not a dichotomy, at least a sharp distinction, when in fact, translating *is* in itself writing, and the translator must, therefore, also be a writer. Which is not to say that the translator must be an a priori self-identified writer outside of his or her translating, for such an assertion would, again, deny translation itself as writing.

This is not to erase the distinction the two words allow, but rather to insist that translation includes both: the text must be translated out of the first language, and then must be written into the second language, so, though we routinely speak simply of translation, that's really only half the process. If it becomes the whole process, i.e., if the work is translated into, rather than written into, the second language, it remains locked to the first, to its rhythms and its syntax, and even more to its deep assumptions, which may be thought of as a deeper rhythm and deeper syntax than those that we change in changing the words—a rhythm and syntax of the mind that sculpts the language rather than those of the language itself. These deeper rhythms, though they can't be isolated or directly perceived, will always leave their traces and cause a haunting; this is excellent—and inevitable. The translator does not need to ensure it through intentionally "foreignizing" aspects, which are often the result of the translator's fear of accidentally appropriating a text by truly writing it into the target language. Yet if the new text remains translated and not written, it will be not so much haunted by as imprisoned in the first language, and will therefore never really arrive, never come alive, in the second.

The "writing into" stage is quite separate from the "translating out of" stage. It requires a different set of questions, all of which address the intangible and untraceable. It's a stage beyond the questions of semantics, beyond even those of tone and style. It's a level that instead faces and must acknowledge the inherent incommensurability of language (of any two languages and even within a given language) that the first stage has successfully denied. Therefore, it must begin with the admission of failure, with the admission that the apparent success of the first stage is illusory—functional, yes, but illusory. Where the translator could claim success, the writer must confront language at that level at which there are no equivalencies, at which language is an assertion of singularities in every respect. And it is there that we encounter the true character, not so much of language, but of *a* language. Which is the character of its people and their history, which they have stored there.

And it's translation that reveals this character, that exposes language as a telescopic palimpsest encoding a culture's values through its finest nuances, which are always inarticulable, composed of impulses too light and small for any physical realization. And though at this point, where translation fails and writing must take over, the writer must admit that the character-that-bears-history cannot be re-created in the second language, she or he can, however, introduce there a slight differential that will allow readers an intimation of that other that cannot be captured, an otherness whose slipperiness aligns it with the uncanny, which thus adds an important dimension that did not exist in the text in its first language and which cannot be gotten into a text except by the differential offered by translation, which is why translation is always also an act of critical acculturation and cultural criticism.

Focusing on these aspects on the one hand and the centrality of writing creatively on the other can keep the translation from becoming domesticated, allowing its foreignization, but with an attention to surface that distinguishes a haunted translation from a merely inept one. In other words, writing into the target language does not mean writing a target-language text; it means putting an emphasis on the writing in order to ensure a work of art.

The influence that translating has on a writer's other writing has everything to do with that haunting by the deep rhythms of other languages. Because translation requires that the text be internalized, these rhythms become a part of the writer's ambient background; they enter into his or her default reservoir. Such internalization makes these influences quite different from those encountered through reading or even analyzing or critiquing, as the internalizing of a text radically changes it, dissolves it into its constituent parts of sound, nuance, motion, etc. In such a dissolved state, these influences are on the one hand more pervasive—they work their way in through the smallest cracks in consciousness—and less perceptible, less identifiable because they arrive in such threads, and mingle, almost on the cellular level, with the other impulses inhabiting the writer.

After several years, a translator becomes awash with others' voices, with subtle shades of other points of view, other approaches that make his or her own more complex. The foreign enters any given language's literature in just this way, importing values and perspectives that gradually estrange a literature from itself, an estrangement that fractures any presumed unity and creates a threat of awkwardness that a literature must continually confront and accommodate through growth and invention. The foreign here is the agent that prevents stagnation. To say it is analogous to the irritant at the core of the pearl would be gushily ornate, but it wouldn't be inaccurate.

The translator is inhabited not only by the specific voices of those that he or she has translated, but also by the deep, silent voice of the cultures whose languages she or he has internalized. Any writer is permeated with influences—that is perhaps the only way our voices can grow and change at all—but the translator's influences are different in that some of them don't fit smoothly because of the collision of these deep structures, assumptions, and traces, and so he or she, like a literature, must also keep the pressure on growth.

The encounter at the base of translation is not only a collision; it's also a conversation, and one that takes place on two levels: the two languages are in a constant conversation that filters, perhaps untraceably, throughout the writer/translator's own creative work, and the two writers are in conversation in subtle and ongoing ways. It's a conversation about literature, but even more important, it's a conversation through literature, using literature—language layered, sculpted, and aestheticized—as the mode of communication. The work joins in the conversation as its condition of possibility. It's also a conversation about poetics, about linguistics, about the nature and potentials of language, and it occurs whether or not the two writers ever meet, whether or not one of them is dead, though the conversation is undoubtedly more intricate in the relatively rare case in which translator and translated actually know each other. Such a case allows the boundaries of the texts to be permeated and the translated text to be informed by friendship. Friendship can be viewed as an overlap, a conceptual zone in which aspects of two people comingle, each retaining his or her own identity while also creating a third entity. In this case, part of that third entity is the translation, and it remains a testimony to an agreement, is the accretion of that agreement. This seems true even in cases in which the writer of the first text is dead and suggests that though a person may die, their capacity for friendship does not, and can in fact, be brought back to life by the interest and appreciation of another.

In Praise of Error

Much thinking on translation is based on the assumption that it has something to do with two languages, but it's not so much a matter of two languages as it is of the gap between them. And far from reducing that gap, translation usually increases it by making us suddenly aware of what cannot be said, not only in the other language, but also in our own, and thus the bottomless silence that is the unsayable grows. In this way, translation makes us aware of a poverty we never before realized we suffered, and we quite naturally resent this. Furthermore, we're made aware not only of what we can't say, but also of nuances of feeling and insight that, through the limitations of our native language, we simply can't attain. These meanings, nuances, and feelings all seem to fall headfirst into the interlingual chasm, ever enlarging it. Thus, though countless grant applications are written every year extolling translation's ability to bridge cultural gaps, it actually only increases them.

Which is potentially good news: when we consider that one of the greatest contemporary threats to vibrant, productive culture is the homogenization resulting from increasing globalization, we see that translation offers great benefits. It maintains particularity, refuses acquiescence, and increases the misunderstandings that linguistic difference so often occasions. And misunderstanding is a greatly underrated, underused resource. At its best, it can result in a neo-understanding that offers a fresh interpretation, a fresh version, which doesn't replace the first, but runs parallel to it, a doppelganger, a *sosie* that doesn't quite fit. It is the guarantor of uniqueness and makes a virtue of incommensurability. Like noise in a system or a genetic mutation, it can augment what was intended, contributing its own details and flair.

And the nice thing about misunderstanding is that you don't need a lot of it. In fact, slight misunderstandings often create the sort of offset that ignites a reverberation. We're more familiar with this in other arts—for instance, the slight offsets that animated much pop art in the 1960s or the haunting undertones and overtones that enrich music—but the same thing occurs in the mental realm: two thoughts that are very close but not quite congruent set up a ringing between them, creating a slight additional dimension that brings them both out more vividly. And is understanding ever exact anyway? Can we ever know, sense, feel precisely what another intended? What we call understanding are simply those instances when the additional meanings are too slight to become conscious or fit so well into our needs and desires of the moment that we don't question them. They slip by unnoticed, and are therefore often wasted. Which is to say that understanding, for the most part, is pretty useless; it adds nothing to the body of human data, but merely repeats an element already in existence. Again, it's in misunderstanding that the promise lies. Which leads us to ask how much difference we can tolerate between utterance and interpretation before we say that understanding has missed.

We can put all this on sound theoretical footing by appealing to information science and its concept of self-organization from noise. (See the title essay of this volume.) The basic concept is a simple one: whenever a message gets transferred from one site to another, whether it's from speaker to listener in a room or over the telephone, or from writer to reader in a book, or from parent to child through DNA, there's always the chance that the message will become altered in the transmission. We tend to think of such alterations as damage, but, as in the case of the alterations to the genetic message that led to the opposable thumb, these alterations are not necessarily bad. Like most things, it depends on what you do with them.

Alterations that occur to a message within the transmission and reception systems are called "noise" (as in the crackling of a "bad connection"), and noise always makes the system more complex, which means that its potential for meaning has increased. To apply this to translation, we have to think of the translation and its source text as a single system, one which also incorporates the writer, translator, and reader. Texts don't operate on their own; they must be involved with these other elements to attain any meaning at all, though it is the text itself that generates the system. Any text's system is always growing; it includes all translations of the text and all other writings on it, as well as all of its readers and their interpretations of it and, eventually, all the effects—thoughts, deeds, etc.—of which it was the instigation.

Even within the artificially simplified version of the system constituted by writer, text, translator, translation, and reader, no message is ever received precisely as sent; instead, a translator is always working in an environment in which meaning is a priori threatened by everything from changes in connotations and references to reader distractibility. To try to be "faithful" in such an environment would require an approach like Pierre Menard's to his *Don Quixote*, in which, through tremendous effort and extreme concentration, he was able to translate Cervantes's classic into an exact copy of itself.[1] That was a case of perfect understanding—and while Borges's description of it added a brilliant short story to world literature, Menard's translation added nothing. The only way to avoid that pitfall is to accept that a certain amount of noise, or difference, will inevitably be incorporated, but that attentive readers will be able to organize that noise into something meaningful.

Children recognize the value of this principle and use it as the basis for the game Chinese Whispers. It delights them because they put a different interpretation on loss. So much thinking in the field of translation is conditioned by the conviction that something is necessarily lost, but this presumption disserves the field and all its projects. For one, it starts the discussion off on a morbid note; writer, translator, and reader enter the scene already dressed in mourning. And it introduces a tinge of nostalgia for "that which is no longer." Both attitudes have us looking backward, not forward, and accepting defeat before we've even begun because that way we have less to live up to in the long run. In the second and more important place, it's inaccurate. Nothing *is* lost; every bit is right there where it has always been, in the source text. It is perfectly safe, and we know right where to find it when we need it. So the translation can afford to lose something, and in fact must lose something, for a translation that loses nothing will not gain anything either. If, however, we regard difference not as loss but as augmentation, we can argue that translation is always an additive gesture, a mechanism for gathering increasing meaning to an ever-expanding text.

This is not to say that we shouldn't cultivate the *illusion* that something is lost, for, like misunderstanding, loss is an abundant resource not to be discounted. The notion that something is lost allows us to enter into the rich and rewarding process of searching for it, which, while not likely to yield the sought-after element, does often cause us to run across other useful and delightful things we never would have thought to look for. Missing things are useful, too, in that they stimulate the imagination. Readers who assume that much has been lost will imagine much more powerful, moving, and lovely things than are likely ever to have been there in the first place. It makes readers stretch their minds an extra measure, as they prefer to risk outdoing the inaccessible original rather than feel like they've missed out on something. Thus what's lost becomes a ghost, a spirit that hovers over the text, an undifferentiated energy that, like stem cells, can be tapped and adapted to meet the needs of the moment.

Misunderstanding and loss are the two principal types of error open to the enterprising translator, for to translate is to err, both in these ways and, perhaps most of all, in the French sense, as in the verb *errer:* to wander, to roam. Translation, like all writing, is intimately linked to walking. Writing is the walking of the mind. Like the walking of the body, it combs through the cells, gets them aligned, and like the body's walking, its essential medium and product is rhythm. It establishes the rhythm that puts the heartbeat and the breath in sync; it keeps time with the outside world.

If all writing is walking, translation is walking of a certain sort, the sort that wanders, meanders; it must take an uncharted course. Original writing carves out a path, which its translation must take, but it must take it without following it; it must take it as though it were raw territory, thus tracing the known, but with the tension and promise of unknowing. Translating is an open-sided walking that demands (and cultivates the faculty for) attention without intention. It demands that one be receptive but not directive, with a sharp ear out for the overtones and under-tones, for the peripheries and margins. It is to err into adjacent regions, which is to make these regions suddenly perceptible.

We tend to think of a text as an isolated instance, as an island of language in midair, when in fact, it is more analogous to an archipelago of certain words lit up within, emerging from the sea of words that surrounds it. Every text exists within a context of reasonable (or unreasonable) assumptions and associations that accompany any word. For instance, you can't have "a wake" without either a boat or a body, though they need not be men-tioned, and if you're deft, you can get both. Boats and bodies in turn bring with them all sorts of other images and territories, and a good translation can wander into some of this territory, making it perceptible and broadening the path of the original.

In his book *Un peuple,* Stéphane Bouquet cites the case of a French translation of Virginia Woolf's *Mrs. Dalloway* in which, toward the end of the party scene, when Mrs. Dalloway is by her-self, thinking of Septimus, the translator has added Mrs. Dal-loway's thought "la morte est une étreinte" (death is an em-brace).[2] It's not in the original, nor in any other translation. It is an error, but above all, it is an errancy. The translator has wan-dered into regions immediately adjacent to the original, regions implied by the original, even made necessary and inevitable by the original. The line was an overtone that this translator heard so loudly that it became audible to us all.

To err from the text is not the same as to err in the text—to err in it simply has us running in circles, creating noise that may or may not be useful, whereas to err *from* the text extends it; it creates space. It is to start with a thread and draw it outward into a world, even if the world is only one phrase long. In the *Mrs. Dalloway* case, it was five words, but beyond that, it was a gener-ative action; it set the text in motion again by establishing within it a new vector that will be further extended in the reader's mind, as it was in Bouquet's when he leapt from there to his own next thought: "elle dit que la mort aussi est un instant de la matière" (she says that death is also a material instant/instant of matter).[3] It is translation and its errant errors that brought that beautiful thought into being. This cannot be wrong.

The word "errant" also evokes the image of the "knight errant": the errant always has something of the Don Quixote about it, and in turn, the sign of Quixote is always hovering over translation, which may be why Borges chose this figure for his seminal speculative work on the subject. Quixote is the patron saint of translation, revealing it as both gallant and foolish, always on the side of right, and always just a little bit wrong. Like Quixote, translation creates a world based on, but not limited to, an independently preexisting one, and like Quixote, it doesn't recognize the difference between the two.

And like Quixote, it is always about to stumble in when uninvited, which is how many translators feel—they feel intrusive, and because of that they refuse to err. They follow the path of the original text very closely, but often this amounts to translating the book *out* of the original language, but not then writing it *into* the target language. Translation doesn't end when the words have been exchanged; it must then start the wandering that will let the new text find its own path. This path is greatly limited, however, by our fetish for semantic meaning. That fetish, or tremendous bias, means that we trust the translator as proxy to choose different sounds but not different senses. It means we consider a text as meaning couched in sound, and not the other way around and not an equal collaboration of the two. And this, of course, makes translating poetry impossible.

NOTES

1. Jorge Luis Borges, "Pierre Menard, Author of the Quixote," in *Labyrinths,* trans. Donald A. Yates (New York: New Directions, 2007), 36–44.
2. Stéphane Bouquet, *Un peuple* (Paris: Champs Vallon, 2007), 10.
3. Ibid., 10.

Translating Timbre

A core issue in translation practice is the proper balance of language's two principal poles, those of sense and of sound. The balance chosen is often uneven, displaying a traditional bias toward sense. This bias presents a problem for poetry, which relies so heavily on sound, and examining the choices that poetry translators actually make reveals that they join in the general bias and routinely sacrifice sound in favor of sense. Poetry translators will at times comment that, though they realize that they're doing the poem as a whole an injustice, they don't feel they have the right to stretch the boundaries of sense in order to accommodate sound.

The use of the word "right" in this context reveals the issue of intellectual property to be lurking at its core, and emphasizes the widespread belief that ideas are separate from the language that conveys them. In fact, we identify thoughts so strongly with their thinker that we assume that the idea simply equals the person. To alter another's idea, we feel, is to alter that other him- or herself. But to alter his or her *sound* is regarded as changing nothing more than a framing device. However, for those who hold that language constitutes rather than conveys its content, this is an issue that needs to be addressed in all translation, not just that of poetry, but because poetry banks so much of its impact in nonsemantic elements, its translation can function as an excellent laboratory for experimenting with ways to salvage sound.

Our bias toward sense in translation is not just an enactment of the "idea = person" equation; it's also an active bias against sound, which, in this case, is based on timorousness; a translator is on much firmer ground with sense than with sound. Sense can be tracked, can be checked, and we can say with certainty whether or not that aspect of the translation is "correct." This isn't true with sound. When we focus on sound, we find ourselves in the unsettling realm of the subjective, where we can't check our work against an objective scale and can't defend ourselves if someone questions our choices.

While in the abstract, I feel strongly that poetry translations should follow sound as much as they follow sense, I understand, and indeed regularly encounter, the difficulties of putting this into practice. In order to explore responsible ways of changing sense in order to accommodate sound, I began translating my own work, which allowed me, as suddenly both translator and poet, to change both sound and sense as seemed appropriate, and to pay close attention to the sensations and decisions that led to my choices. My work happens to be good for this kind of exploration because it is heavily based on sound. Often the choices I make in writing the original English poem are based on rhythm, rhyme, assonance, and other sound relationships as much or more than on meaning—or perhaps it's more accurate to say that the meaning is often in the sounds of the words and phrases as much as it is in their definitions. Occasionally the sound has a degree of specific meaning; for instance, a languid rhythm might support a languid image, or a rhyme might underscore a semantic parallel or opposition, but that's actually pretty rare; most often, the meaning of the sounds is the sounds themselves.

I began these translations as I usually begin translations—with the background assumption that sound and sense are the two major poles in play and that they operate in a constantly complementary relationship. However, when I began to pay attention to my actual thought processes in choosing new French content to replace the English in order to preserve sound, I found that I wasn't choosing the new content just to fit the new sound requirement, but that I was paying attention to a third quality, equal in importance to the other two, but less overtly apparent, one that I thought of at times as the word's tone or integrity. For instance, the word "mansion" would not need to be replaced by a kind of dwelling, but it would have to be replaced by something—either concrete or abstract—that has a touch of the vast in its senses of airy and distant. It couldn't be replaced by something, say, focused or ironic or technical, no matter how appropriate the sound, and it couldn't be replaced by the same thing that, for instance, "house" would be replaced by—that would require something intricate, intimate, and encompassing, no matter at what scale.

The quality I found myself tracking feels quite specific, even if it isn't precisely nameable, describable, or locatable. It's a quality internal to both the word's materiality and its concept (perhaps it's even what fuses the two), and it seems to be sheer quality, in that it is unquantifiable and cannot be compared with others of its sort in a hierarchical relationship. Writers deal with such sheer quality all the time, but the translator is much more likely to make quantitative decisions or to try, to some degree, to convert quality into quantity in order to have a more definite basis for the translation.

I came to think of this third quality as timbre. It functions as a third pole in the translation dynamic—and in the poetic dynamic—a pole that is even more elusive than sound. Ironically, by bringing something into the mix that is even harder to track, I found that I could get a firmer grip on the suddenly relatively-less-slippery pole of sound. Timbre is considered slippery even in music, which is where the concept is most frequently used. In fact, it's often defined in the negative. I heard it explained recently as the quality that allows you to tell a flute from an oboe when they're both playing the same note at the same volume for the same length of time. Or what lets you discern Pavarotti's voice from Domingo's when they're both singing the same thing. It's what's left when you've removed all other, all traceable, musical parameters. (Which can't help but evoke Frost's "poetry is what gets lost in translation.") Even dictionaries define timbre, if not negatively, at least vaguely, for instance, Webster's: "the distinctive property of a complex sound," and "the quality or tone distinguishing voices or instruments," and while some people in the business offer elaborations such as "Timbre is a multidimensional perceptual attribute of complex tones that characterizes the identity of a sound source," they don't necessarily get much more specific. Many writings on the structure of music refer to it as "the color of music," which, while evoking something very helpful, also admits that the concept is not readily delimitable or concretely definable. Technically, it's a product of overtones;

each musical instrument sets up different overtones, as does each voice—and each word. As recent work in the neuroscience of reading has shown, when we hear or see a word, we think not just of that word but also instantly of many, many others that form of a field of associations around it.[1] This property is particularly exploited in poetry, where associative wandering and a high level of ambiguity are both extremely productive.

The larger and more active the field of overtones around each word becomes, the more it engages the reading mind, which at times holds dozens of possibilities in suspension at once, all the while following a denotative line through them. The relative sizes of the denotative line and the field of overtones are important; when fields are huge, the line may be relatively small, and therefore not as crucial to follow precisely when translating because it constitutes a smaller percentage of the meaning's whole. An extreme example of this would be an abstract poetry that uses vivid words in illogical sequences, preventing denotations from accumulating into a coherent message; at the other extreme, narrative poetry with little ambiguity and little sound play would present a denotative line that is very large in relation to its fields of overtones, requiring a translation that relies heavily on sense. Being aware of timbre is in part a matter of being aware of these fields of overtones and their relative roles.

It's also a matter of realizing how complex the denotative line is, of recognizing more than referential definitions, of validating other aspects, such as the emotive, and others too elusive to name. By using timbre to complicate the notion of definition, a translator can alter content in ways that both honor sound and conserve the integrity of the text.

I'd like briefly to return to an issue addressed earlier, that of the general bias, at least in the western world, for sense over sound. I remarked that I thought it was not only a bias toward sense, but one against sound, which can, inadvertently, amount to a bias against aesthetics. Without intending it, and without even realizing it, we often treat the aesthetic as something to be accommodated only if there are resources—time, energy, imagination, money—left over. The aesthetic is seen as excess, and excess is understood as superfluous. Though we give it lip service, in fact, we treat the aesthetic as decorative, a term which has, in turn, been reduced to mean "inessential, performing no function," which reflects our general bias toward that which has a function and our disdain for that which (seemingly) does not—we're a pragmatic culture, and that may or may not be a good thing, but, be that as it may, we're wrong about aesthetics; it is not without function. Recent work in the neuroscience of aesthetics has demonstrated its role in the development of the brain. In particular, it seems that the visual arts may train the brain to create representational distillations of the outside world, effectively bridging inside and out.[2] Though most work in neuro-aesthetics focuses on visual art and music, clearly all art has an impact on the brain, and I think poetry has a special role. Though it would be speculation, we might consider not only that poetry works on representational strategies in a very different way than other arts, but that it also lets both poet and reader strengthen memory and exercise metaphoric thinking, which some have argued is central to positioning ourselves in the world.[3] And some studies have indicated that when the brain processes rhythm in music, it activates Brodmann areas 44 and 45 (more commonly known as Broca's area) and 22 (Wernicke's area), which are central, respectively, to the production and the understanding of language.[4] The confluence of rhythm and language points to poetry, and though, again, this is speculation, poetry may help the brain carry out a wide range of functions, from recognizing patterns, managing balance, and dealing creatively with imbalance to coming to terms with time.

Supposing, for argument's sake, that poetry does have these qualities; what then might translation add to them? For one, while translating poetry challenges the brain in the above ways, just as reading poetry would, it simultaneously imposes the need for rational thinking. Because the translator must not only translate, but also write, translation requires the openness to the irrational required by all creative activity and yet the attention to the rational required by all analysis. This blend of skills comes up in few other activities and perhaps strengthens the cooperation between these two very different ways of thinking, which may in turn incite a third, entirely new, way of using the mind.

Appendix

The following is an example of a poem self-translated in order to explore this question of timbre. First written in English, it was then translated into French, and then translated back into English.

After This Death There Will Be No Other[5]

Some say a child
        becomes the house
               some houses hold
                       the child in hand
in the heart of a bird
             is its hollow home
                   that green flight
that lets the house lose form
           where was the room
                why a door to the air
why air in the eye
        and why only sky where
               the child held the house
in the palm of her hand
        and the sky
            poured over it, painting her out.

Il y a ceux qui disent qu'un enfant
        devient la maison.
            il y a des maisons
qui tiennent
     l'enfant par la main
        dans le coeur d'un oiseau
            est un navire
qui mene
    un vol à vif jusqu'a une maison en miettes
           où était la chambre

pourquoi l'ombre impaire
        et pourquoi la defaire
                l'enfant a mis une maison
dans la paume de sa main
        et le ciel l'effacé
             en la rendant errante

There are those who say
        child turns to house
             there are houses that take
the child by the hand
        and heart-bird of bell-rope
             what ship do you have
flying green till the house falls down from the home
           where was the room?
               why
the shadow on call?
        and why do you keep on trying, my loss?
           the child put the house
in the palm of her hand
        and the sky filled it up
           with the sky burning down.

NOTES

1. Maryanne Wolf, *Proust and the Squid* (New York: Harper Collins 2007), 9.

2. For instance, Terrence Deacon, "The Aesthetic Faculty," and Merlin Donald, "Art and Cognitive Evolution," both in *The Artful Mind,* ed. Mark Turner (Oxford and New York: Oxford University Press, 2006), 23 and 4 respectively; Irving Massey, *The Neural Imagination* (Austin: University of Texas Press, 2009), passim; Semir Zeki, *Inner Vision* (Oxford and New York: Oxford University Press, 2000), passim.

3. George Lakoff and Mark Johnson, *Metaphors We Live By* (Chicago: University of Chicago Press, 1980), passim.

4. Joyce L. Chen, Virginia B. Benhune, et al., "Listening to Musical Rhythms Recruits Motor Regions of the Brain," *Cerebral Cortex,* Dec. 2008.

5. This title is a slight modification of the last line of Dylan Thomas's poem "A Refusal to Mourn the Death, by Fire, of a Child in London."

Translating the Visible

The Incommensurability of Image

Translation has been claimed by many to be the deepest way of reading—and could it not also be the deepest way of seeing? Three issues related to translation offer ways into this question: image, emergence, and the ghostly. Works by two contemporary French writers, Caroline Dubois's book *C'est toi le business*[1] (*You Are the Business*[2]) and Suzanne Doppelt's *Le pré est vénéneux*[3] (*The Field Is Lethal*[4]), though very different in style and theme, offer vital examples of the issues embedded in translating image, as well as an opportunity to look at translation's relation to emergence. And here I don't mean the word in the scientific sense, but in the more commonplace sense of something that is not quite entirely present, but that is moving toward presence and carries with it that momentum and that potential, as well as the pressure, the slight anxiety, of potential whose realization cannot be predicted. Translation, in a sense, is always emergent, in that once it has fully emerged, it's no longer translation; it's a text.

But for the moment, image: Dubois's book is based on a series of films, so the problem of translation is already central— the problem of translating from one medium into another. And Dubois does this gracefully and concisely, translating the emotional impact of visual material through insinuation and association into a similarly emotionally moving work in the completely different medium that is language. And, as the original medium is entirely based on image, Dubois must keep that image-ness somehow foregrounded in her work, which she does, but in her work the images are necessarily hidden in that they are masked by the very language that presents them. Readers access them *through* the language only, while they remain inside the text, interior to it, down somewhere deep in its imaginary.

For instance, a passage such as "So Blade Runner in order to make the words come whose source she doesn't know come out of her mouth is forced to rough her up a little to push her into the venetian blinds with a certain violence"[5] not only contains but is entirely dependent upon the striking image at the end. The film *Blade Runner* was sufficiently popular that Dubois can assume that its images are shared by a significant number of her readers. This was a particularly vivid image in the movie, and most of us in reading that passage will reproduce it in our heads. But two things are crucial here. First, that image will be entirely private—generated by a public medium, but deeply privatized by being stored in individual memories where it mingles with private recollections and associations and is subject to the modifications that individual memories make—forgetting certain details, emphasizing personally meaningful aspects, etc., so that the image becomes an internal one, and our being reminded of it here reinforces the commonplace practice of assimilating images from the public sphere.

The second issue, and the one that particularly concerns the translator, is that the image occurred in English, which is to say that it occurred originally in an English-language cultural context, in an English-language movie; thus, even though an image is a nonlinguistic object, we can, and must, say that it occurred in English—and that the fact that an image has a native language is important. One of the things that Dubois has done in her book is to translate the image from English into French by transferring it to a French context. And here context takes on a very narrow meaning because the environment has so dramatically changed. The environment now is entirely linguistic, and the language is French. This means that what the translator must do is not so much translate it back into English, as, in fact, *un*translate it.

The problem of untranslation is further compounded by the fact that the book includes many quotations, translated into French from the movies that are its subjects, many of which were made in English, and whose English lines remain in the ear of the French public. Such quotations translated into French set up a dynamic activity, a constant oscillation between English and French, building a differential into the French text, in which the French is read, but within and against a background of an English that is heard/remembered, thus overheard. Because Dubois chooses lines that are well-known to moviegoers, and from well-known movies, the attuned French reader gets a curious stereophonic mismatch, which adds a linguistic dimension: the French reader hears and understands simultaneously the "same thing" made different within itself. This dynamic of doubling/decalage cannot exist in the English version, and there's no way to recuperate the lost effect by other means. Instead, again, I have to untranslate what she has so masterfully translated. And the untranslating process is itself interesting—it requires hours and hours of going back through the movies she's referencing, trying to catch certain lines in order to transcribe them, which means that my translation at that point flips into transcription, and the emergence of another's text (the screenwriter's) into my own creates a surface texture unavailable to the original.

These verbally/visually ambiguous images come up all through the book; for instance, in a sequence based on the movie *The Miracle Worker,* we read: "When I cry when I touch mamma's mouth I don't know if I cry in fact I mean like cry like mamma or is it something else."[6] Again, the film is sufficiently well-known to raise the image in the minds of most readers with all the modifications inherent in memory. The ironies of visibility/invisibility are all the more underscored here as we find ourselves looking simultaneously at and from the perspective of someone who is blind.

The image of the mouth recurs throughout the book, and particularly the image of words coming out of the mouth, which emphasizes the visibility/invisibility dynamic in that we are caused to picture something invisible, and in fact, in our mind's eye, we can see this invisibility precisely—and only because the medium at hand, language, by its very inability to show it, is relieved of the obligation. And as such, the image never completely arrives, never becomes concrete, but hovers there in the mind in an ever-emergent state.

Emergence, the concept of and the state of, is key for translation in a number of ways, and I'm going to describe an image that illustrates at least a part of this: I often write the initial draft of a translation in pencil directly into the published original, sketching in my version "between the lines," as it were. This has the effect of turning the published book into a workbook, of unsettling its finished surface, but it also has the sheerly practical advantage of relieving me of the obligation of going back and forth between two surfaces, and allows me to translate wherever I am, provided that I have the book with me. The resulting object is thus a text printed in black ink with an interlineal annotation in a paler pencil. And though it may seem to be simply an accident of the way I happen to work, I think there's something actual going on under the visual pun: against and in between the black text of the original, we see the translation emerging, less definite in both density and form—less dense because it is in pencil; parts of it will be erased, and then rewritten; it is still in flux. And its form is less definite because handwriting is not as locked into shape as type is, but instead reflects the fluctuations of mood and moment. This is the only point at which the emerging text is actually a translation; in this moment between the original text and the final "translated" product, we can see them still linked, still intimately related to each other in a kind of conversation, a kind of call and response, in which they listen to and construct each other.

And because this stage is executed in handwriting rather than in print, it transforms the entire page, both "original" and "translation," into visual art, and that leap into the visual fuses the two in a way that translation and original are never otherwise joined. Even a face-en-face publication cannot achieve this fusion because the fact of their both being in print fixes them in their typeblocks; interaction is no longer possible, but as long as handwriting is still involved, the event overflows into visual art, and not because of the "handmade" quality of handwriting, or any notion of its "beauty," or the aura of the hand, etc., but because of the gap, the decalage between the print and the hand. It's the gap and the necessity it incites to leap it that transform it into visual art, which allows the two linguistic gestures to become a single move; in other words, the same gap exists between an original and a translation.

The central issue of emergence in translation is well illustrated by another book I've translated. Like Dubois's book, *Le pré est vénéneux* by Suzanne Doppelt contains images that call the basic assumptions of translation into question, though here the images are entirely exterior—on the one hand, they have completely emerged from the text and exist beside it as photographs, and on the other, they are unprecedented images; they can't rely on shared memory; they are completely externalized as events occurring outside the reader, outside the writer, outside the text. They have no "inner life" or iconic baggage, as do images in a film, which always bring the past along with them; instead, these reverberate outward from the page, new images heading out into a future. Some of her images can be seen if you search under her name at http://www.pol-editeur.com and then view the PDFs of the beginning pages of her books.

The irony here is that these images can't be translated, and while their immediacy might tempt one to think that they don't need to be translated, in fact, they must be because they, too, were greatly changed when all the linguistic elements of the book surrounding them changed, just as Dubois's images changed when their environment did. And yet, you look at them in Doppelt's book and then in the published translation, and they're exactly the same, so as a translation project, it's a complete failure.

While that would be true of any project with this image/text relationship, these particular images even further complicate the discussion, for while they remain wholly exterior, they resist complete emergence, complete arrival, because, for the most part, they refuse to be images *of* anything, and yet we're aware that there was an object somewhere in their process that won't quite materialize; the very imaging of it has masked that object, insisting instead on an immanent untransferability, which constitutes another level of their untranslatability.

The sharp contrasts between the images on a given page also let them work by dynamic shift, similar to that between the implicitly bilingual layers of Dubois's text. This contrast creates an oscillation, as if the image itself were unsteady, a stereoscoping that refuses to resolve into a smooth, dimensionalized image. Instead we are made acutely aware of the seams, which in turn direct our attention to the construction of the text, which uses many collaged elements all rather boldly stitched together and interspersed with Doppelt's interpretations and extensions. So while, like Dubois's, Doppelt's project is one of mining various sources, Doppelt doesn't use quotations directly. Instead she takes the materials and transforms them into ghostly echoes of their earlier forms. This ghostliness overflows into content; in fact, the book takes ghosts and ghostly phenomena—séances, ventriloquism, magic carpets, apparitions—as its subject, capitalizing on these inherently emergent phenomena, which hover, like translations, between two worlds.

NOTES

1. Caroline Dubois, *C'est toi le business* (Paris: P.O.L, 2005).

2. Caroline Dubois, *You Are the Business,* trans. Cole Swensen (Providence: Burning Deck Publications, 2008).

3. Suzanne Doppelt, *Le pré est vénéneux* (Paris: P.O.L, 2007).

4. Suzanne Doppelt, *The Field Is Lethal,* trans. Cole Swensen (Denver: Counterpath Press, 2010).

5. Dubois, *You Are the Business,* 15.

6. Ibid., 66.

The Ghost of Translation

Once the poet has properly embodied his most
fleeting emotion in the most appropriate words, then
this emotion will continue to live on through these
words for millennia and will flourish anew in every
sensitive reader.
—Schopenhauer, translated by Peter Mollenhauer

Schopenhauer's comment implies that to write is to cast yourself beyond death, which is to cast yourself out of life, which, as
language constructs that thought, lands us in a liminal zone between these two extremes, which is what we've traditionally regarded as the realm of ghosts.

If we think of a ghost:

1. as a doubling through the trace, as the vestige, seized,
   of something or someone with which one would have
   been more at ease; as an occupation, as an inhabiting
   of these
2. as a shadow-double made somehow of light, doppelganger, in others made shy. The fleeting is the ghost, is
   that which tries to grip, and slips. It's off on its own,
   griefly flitting past the corner of the eye,
3. as that thing through which you pass, troubled by its degree of absolute substance, yet, if it functions, you look
   right through to what is no longer there, and that will
   abyss.

Each of these is also a description of translation. And follows
the ghost into all its contradiction: a ghost speaks without showing its face, a disembodied voice with no coordinates in space:
the translation emanates from the now-silenced text.

Or the face arrives alone and you have to invent the words: translation planing just above the field, describing in its dips and turns the contours of the landscape below. Ghosts are often described by their motion rather than by their form—something gliding up a stair, an undulation on the threshold.

Translation imagines the words through which it will, in an impressionable moment, a weak moment, a moment when the door is left open, and the sun comes in allowing you to see right through something in the middle of the room, speaking, and you don't know the language, but the poem is there.

A translation is a ghost: it goes out into another world in all its perfect viability; it causes belief, while on the other hand, it sets up an echo, very faint, in the original, so that the original is now haunted by a separate voice that continues to separate. A ghost is always offset, slightly incongruent, and fraying at the edge: a translation, unlike an original, can never stop, it bleeds on out; it causes changes in itself.

A ghost is a layering of transparencies to such a depth that nothing ever goes away.

Of keeping literature as a train, as a chain, as an *enchaînement* dragging history into a propulsive state, the sheer weight of reverberation among language upon language because language innately harbors the dead; it gathers them along with it, hauls them forward into it, and so hauls forward all its history of nuance and deviation.

Each time a text is translated, it gains another ghost that lives within, ventriloquist, is only heard beyond itself, and no matter how much that text lives on, its ghost will always precede it, traveling where the text itself has no business.

The ghost is also all that language cannot say or refuses to say—which haunts alongside every poem and is only compounded by translation, for one translates not only the words, but also their failures. And they, unlike the words, cannot be erased, cannot ever be altered. And unable to pass into representation, will remain ever more present, but untraceable. And will hold you accountable.

If to write is to foreshadow your own death, and to cast a line out beyond its limit, then to translate is to step into the death of another, and become therefore doubly a stranger. We bother the dead by arriving early and unprepared. A noise in another room, shuffling papers. They turn around to emptiness. Whose guest

or we always speak a reverberatory tongue, and once written down, it does nothing but collect. Translation just adds another mechanism of augmentation, but one that then takes on its own life and travels haunted by the very text it abandoned through its enactment.

Translation is a catalogue of loss. Which further translations—into other languages or other versions—will attempt to attenuate, but will instead accentuate. It's the ghosts that grow, and we now think there may have been, must have been, the living once, who cast no reflections.

NOTE

Arthur Schopenhauer, "On Language and Words," trans. Peter Mollenhauer, in *Theories of Translation,* ed. Rainer Schulte and John Biguenet (Chicago: University of Chicago Press, 1992), 32.

Homages

All words in italics in this section are taken from the work of the subject of the piece, though most have been taken out of context, arranged differently, or spliced in among each other.

For M. Moore

Such animals as
All over   word
               wish
               if
               after
It alters
or: its afters only altar with such minute meanders
we know it changed her, that she left altered
that she lived altered and left here

is all this is all of the animal. It's almost locked in place, a pacing and a perpendicular heaven that hasn't, that has not, that
does not have

fish   chameleon   wasp   weather   must
winter the horse, the housing of the carp, carapace of concern
concerning her concentric love for vermin, the ermine, the asp.
Wasp won't thee but will will

forgetting that there is in woman
a quality of mind
which as an instinctive manifestation
is unsafe,
       and wonders just for whom, what him and how soon
                       but that it would
soon
turn.

I think we love people for what they love. Ms. M. and her pocket
zoo, heart made of zippers, opening out like one of those

makeup cases women take travelling that expand in all directions. Consider the opossum. I can't picture Marianne Moore wearing makeup. Ms. Moore did not wear makeup. Consider the horse, the mouse, the house that gets contorted into a heart. Ms. Moore did not go in much for travel. A few times to Europe, a few times west and her hat there at the end of her hand and her hand, all hasp

to so many perhaps   you know first

what the creature's named and then you hold—how many of them had she held? Not the giraffe, the elephant, the bat in broad daylight, the bat, all mouse with its own elaborated gift and its own horse and out there in the sun.

1.: Early on, invented forms. Take, for instance, the fish.: *wade / through black jade / an / injured fan.*

Precise, planned to step like a spine, so rigorous and diligence never counts but exactly knows. To be read whole or first "lines" only or the first two. At times caving/curving in, symmetrically, like the spine of a well-read book seen end-on: "Injudicious Gardening," "To a Chameleon," or steadily, unpredictably laddering, "Critics and Connoisseurs," "To the Peacock of France." Let it precise, pare off any end and in it nip.

"I was trying to be honorable and not steal things."
(is governed by gravity)
"Words cluster like chromosomes, determining the procedure."
(like symmetry)

if honor be
exactitude, an implication of biology and warily, a splice of light that spares the selves, that pares the rest to emergent else. Where then find strife? And what then bind through stealth?

2.: Rhyme, wound tight; spring in the step, fight in the clock and often off: "craven/frighten/certain"; "waist/crest"; they tighten: "star/hair"; "enough/proof"; "faith/death." Again, whose, and yes, but again but whom? (the proof was partial and the faith given conquered:

> *God be praised for conquering faith . . .*   2.5: *"I like*
Gilbert & Sullivan." Inseparable directions

with unequal determinations and inclinations that will not rest innumerous. Will conquer us. G. M. Hopkins brings in tea.

How often do you think she had tea? I've always thought frequently, but now feel I may be or at least must have been entirely aggrieved. She could have done anything with the butt ends of her afternoons.

She haunted the Brooklyn Zoo. This we know. But we don't know what she thought. How much was shock. It should have been all, and it was, if nothing else, not.

Octopus.
Snail
Eight-fold
Owl.
Mouse-skin bellows.
Ostrich.
Ghost.

Cast an own. Come an ox. Add a wild (a feral) truce, a Persian thought, an unidentified Bordeaux.
Holding equal court with Ben Jonson, Jackie Robinson, Captain John Smith, and Melchior Vulpius.

She was angrier than you would have thought from the pictures. A few spare anamorphic constructions and "To Military Progress" and perfectly happy in New York.
we've grown apart

though half the word is after
when asked at the age of twenty
what she'd like to be, she answered
a painter.

gold thread from straw and have heard men say:
"There is a feminine temperament in direct contrast to ours,

Which makes her do these things. shift of chin. the eye
slips on. Someone enters the library in a wedge of light,
a shower of dust *(If I, like Solomon, . . .*
could have my wish—

"What I write, as I have said before, could only be called poetry because
there is no other category in which to put it."

I was recently reading an essay in which the author went to great
lengths to establish Marianne Moore as an "American poet"—or
rather was using her particularities, her eccentricities really
(which should have defeated his point right there), to sketch a
floorplan of "American-ness." I wonder if she would have noticed, though it mattered, thought it existed. Liked England, it's
said. Oh yes. (My brother, the doctor.) (My mother, the dead.)
It's its hardness, all that solid ground, the concrete both and not
metaphorical that's supposed to be so American, the quick twist,
brisk thrust, trust. She moved through her world on rust. Who
would ever know if this (what am I saying) is truth or just, or if
the air in Sweden is sweeter as she says or if the ermine really
would rather be dead

than spotted.
> *Chameleon.*
> *Fire laid upon*

She's walking across a room

an emerald as long as an ire.

She's walking across a room with an inverted glass in her hand
and in the glass, a spider, escorting it "home," sealed at the bottom, of course, with a postcard.
From whom.   A three-cornered hat. A hat with three corners that, in my mind

she is always connected with Joseph Cornell. It's the love of things that's common. Or the love of the loss of as well as the loss of and the sense of love as an intransitive verb. Collect cows, dolls, matchbooks, matches, spiders, crows, I think she had a "thing" about "home."

She's walking across a room. It's dinnertime. Who are the logical (the inevitable) guests? Table for four. She says she said: Joseph Cornell, Emily Dickinson, Gerard de Nerval, and Marianne Moore. But Marianne is late tonight, more spiders than usual or the elephants uncommonly insistent. Natural habitat: botanical gardens, dimestores, (Joe at elbow, suggesting this or that). Definitely the type to poise rubber snakes in cupboards, laundry baskets. Tried it on E. Dickinson, who cried when she touched it and found it wasn't real.
But sound curved
a hand
holding a hand that's holding a hand. What do you call them?
"Experiments in rhythm, exercises in composition."

and what do you mean by enough.

Let us.

3.: *for love that will gaze an eagle blind.* If blindness be fusion, there and only there was decision. Not in the above quotation the invention of the verb. Animals with moving fur. The blur of animals in motion. Blinding. If sight incites distinction, discretion, dissection. (Gerard is shaking his head, saying, "No, this is not a pet")

that we here have built

(in which there are hounds with waists
I must not wish
it comes to this
lit
with piercing glances into the life of things

"My interest in La Fontaine originated entirely independent of content."

I have always wanted
to enter

a room and find the animals
already there and staring
out the windows.

Besides, of Bedouins—On *Hotel Lautréamont* by John Ashbery

A hotel is distinguished by its many rooms, and a room always stands for a moment of the mind, so every collection of poetry is necessarily a hotel, a sequence of spaces threaded in and above, and therein we live, in passing, in a corridor, in what brushes by your sleeve, the underscore of breath.

This is wealth, and we're just passing through, as they say, there we are and then are not, another stranger, and there's something clean in that. *And to those whose loneliness / shouts envy in my face,* it's a state of pure sunlight, pared of memory, and it's a dream; it's *the* dream: to be seen from the back, walking away until the seer fades, and the reader is left with an open book.

Hotel Lautréamont traces an exile—an ambulatory self-exile in both senses of the term: of the voluntarily chosen, deeply wanted, and escorted, and of the self that walks out on the self until it runs out of land:

> *There is nothing to do except observe the horizon,*
> *the only one, that seems to want to sever itself*
> *from the passing sky.*

Which is passing behind

                      a screen on which a shadow-play keeps time with the gate swinging back and forth of the face, of the name.

Lautréamont was a man who abandoned his name for another of a fictional character from a 19th-century sensationalist novel that no one now remembers how to write the self away and make a dubious hero splinter into the actual. Isidore Ducasse, the author forever on the outside, and Maldoror, the character forever trapped within, meet in this name of another on the cover that divides one world from the next. Lautréamont exiled himself from himself, leaving his native Montevideo to go to Paris to die of the siege.

And Joseph Cornell was an exile from and within his native land and never left New York. You can exile inside; you can build room after very small room with the many addresses of repeated objects. Exiled himself into a small red ball, a grid of white, the repeated word "Hotel."

Seen on a bench this morning: a man in a gray coat is always a photograph in black and white, and the stranger is innumerable and inhabitable, in a soft hat, quietly sealed. "Still Life with Stranger" is full of bees and snow.

Ashbery speaks of *those homeless hirsutes we call men;* this is his homage to them. We see a walking line silhouetted against the horizon, letter for letter, person for person, counting in his sleep, if poetry does not keep track, there will be no more ceremony to this loss and

> *if we are to be more than music*
>
> be erased. It is this

we will interrogate. The erased conveys its passing through a split-second of unclarity, a cloud across the surface, and the paper is no longer virgin. It's a white rectangle with a smudge that looks a little like the condensed breath of someone who had been standing at the window.

From the outside, a hotel is no more than a pattern of windows, often all the same, counters in a game of concentration, and you will never be able to remember where you saw each one before.

Ashbery also exiled himself to Paris where he fell in love with the work of Raymond Roussel, than whom no better monument to alienation both self and universal has ever been conceived. There *is* all that outside. It *does* extend in all directions becoming infinitely more grand and infinitely more precise, and always and essentially without depth. Which was the world he built and into which he fled and lived forever among his simple magic and unlikely machines.

That these three men—Lautréamont, Roussel, and Cornell—are the same one is a law of physics that may seem to have no purpose until it emerges as this book: *great rivers run into each other and graves*
Digression:
That is, of course, a gross misreading of the line or is it. The lines run:
we will meet on a stone up there, and all will not be well,
but that is useful. Great rivers run into each other and graves
have split open, the tyranny of dust plays well, there is
so little to notice. Besides we have always known each other.

And so, because of the line break, we can claim "great rivers run into each other and graves" as a legitimate unit, but more important, this sequence exemplifies Ashbery's device of rarely letting lines conform to the units of sense; they are always carefully offset. This forces the line break to break sense open, to reveal its chasm; while on the other hand, when meaning, as it so often does in Ashbery, achieves its end in the middle of the line, it similarly ruptures that structure; these ends unended, the grave has split, and if something comes alive again because of it, it is this unease that pushes onward, which is the exile inherent in language, now relieved of all constraint. Ashbery's lines will not stay put, but restlessly wander from humor to mourning, resting only a moment suspended as each line breaks into another room with a door at each extreme.

The implications of the hotel are endless, arcanely transient, archly anonymous, always pushing tomorrow off somewhere else. By the time you get there, a hotel room is always empty. In 1981, Sophie Calle spent three weeks as a chambermaid constructing portraits of the hotel guests, portraits constructed in and of their absence, built of the haphazard evidence of daily objects, detritus, traces, until the person in their lack becomes enormous. This we call the present.

And it is constructed of dream. Hotel rooms are permanently permeated with dream. If it is thought that dreams stain the air, and they do, then in hotels they're layered in among strangers because they must build from night to night, are never the product of a single night's work but must wait, leaving those who live in hotels to create a composite mind shared with everyone else who has recently passed through.

To build a mind of the never-met. Ashbery's work is always an exchange of dream, which is a turning from the door every time and every room that glides alone, uncompromising the view, as wrote the Surrealists for whom, like Lautréamont, Roussel, and Cornell, and regardless of timing, Ashbery was a precursor, living there a second time, a graceful loop *autonomous as the birds' song, the vultures' sleep.* You sing and I'll weep. Birds inhabit the person, and the exile is complete. Which is itself in silence, in coming into possession of the self, must be exiled from all else, becoming sovereign, a renovated conference of the birds:

Noon intersects with fat birds: rain of, who won, and winning, rain of oblivion, sudden as a sigh. In the bird, Ashbery and Cornell pass and brush, lightly their hands: aerial Bedouin, migration that does not return with the season.

on a forgotten afternoon filled with birds; wings

        How the forgetting, too, plays into his economy of loss; there is just one spot
on the horizon, and it may or may not have been
the one living thing that always is

        the past. Of it we *build*
individual habitats for bird and person

        The smallest home is a thimble until it is a needle, famous for being nearly all window, and what of the air-balloon, and what are Cornell's boxes if not exits? And how do you tell a bird from a stone? The answer to the riddle had something to do with a pale blue egg upside down.

        There was no season.
We found a homogeneous weather composed entirely of ritual objects. Here he and Cornell confer:

        feather? and if so, how related to snow? and exactly how to manifest this emptiness in such a crowded place. How inexorably to state *the birds were here once,* borrowed
from Uccello, who also

        earned his name from absent birds, birds he painted that no one now can find, *we know* is just the

beginning
of *they were*

once of the interwoven, when after all, they got away, and the shore repeats because the body is a finite thing and Ashbery finds this sad. He is right, and so intricately so in positioning the grief at the point at which man and bird meet, which is the hotel, half-arm, mid-beak, the fulcrum between a bird's foot, which can only be called a claw, and its wing. There is no thing that does not mean. And Ashbery, dedicated to contingency, here constructs a deep mourning for just that inability.

We move continually outward along a chain of islands, ever alien:

Do pigeons flutter? Is there a strangeness there, to complete the one in me?

And of what shape, what silhouette crossed the yard and odd in peace did shed a peace in the dark within the body lies the bird
as whatever's left of flight:

. . . the heart flies a little away,
perhaps accompanying, perhaps not. Perhaps a familiar spirit,
possibly a stranger, a small enemy

Ashbery's first aspiration was to be a painter, and curving outward, with his hand upon the snow in an untitled collage
by Joseph Cornell. There was no Hotel Lautréamont among the prodigious series Cornell constructed in the 1950s.

. . . And when it was over, that was the truth:
a nest of eggs still hidden, the false flight of a bird.

Ashbery's exile is positive, the fulfillment of a promise, the reconciliation with a stranger who never faces you, but keeps looking onward, drawing you out. In his configuration, exile is the refusal to be rendered homeless by constituting that home everywhere.

Exile in style, too. While in *Reported Sightings*, Ashbery writes, "The genius of Cornell is that he sees and enables us to see with the eyes of childhood, before our vision got clouded by experience," he also says that he was shocked when he first saw Cornell's work in a magazine at the age of ten—shocked because Cornell was seeing what no child ever naturally would, and delivered in a rush all the psychological insight of thirty years' experience; to sense the extension of the self as a serial dislocation (*only a lining / that dictates the separation of this you from this some other*), and the fact that the elements of a personality can be freely recombined as a type of flight should be shocking indeed to a child of ten.

And that fact, once internalized, became Ashbery's principle of composition by cumulative juxtaposition, which carves up every on-toward through a neat exchange of metaphor for metonymy, a chain of associations that begin and begin and begin again. In haunted stanzas, we start with rain, then rowboats, then a harpsichord shelling peas. Then darkness. Then:

Happiness no longer was a thing to hold on to, but became a great curve, listening instead

is the entire oeuvre: the darkness necessary to the intelligence of happiness, which must curve, as must a wing, and both must exceed the frame of the mind, turning to pure motion, and all of it, the listening that sends our attention elsewhere still.

Archipelago. It is a book of ships:

that excited skiff

or schooner with its layered sails that climb like clouds; there are so many ways out, but among them, sail and wing are mostly ancient. Ocean vessels, convey-ness hither. He expands on the theme: flotsam and jetsam and their fine distinctions, what we toss overboard, memory and meter, to make the ship lighter and lighter, it's practically floating, it's learning to fly. Thereby becoming the point that wanders free of a line, and often contrasted with its opposite: all buildings that are not hotels, and that therefore hold us down:

And so in turn he who gets locked up is lost
too, and must watch a boat nudge the pier
outside his window, forever, and for aye,

is that wide inviting; we picture it wooden, its paint peeling and an oar of sun aslant its emptiness, a rope in the bottom, coiled.

. . . and the little house more sensible than ever before
as a boat passes, acquiescing to
the open, the shore . . .
the shores are still beautiful
                    they always are
because they're in mid-air; they've got nothing to do with the
ironic earth but mark its edge and own their sails and are sailing.
the ship was obliged to leave for the islands—it doesn't matter which ones.
They all came along
                    . . . you know how we keep an eye on
today. It left on a speeding ship. As everything eventually Isidore
Ducasse got on board and sailed right out of his life.

And when you died
they remembered you chiefly. It was two
lights on a rowboat, a half-mile off shore

Second digression into formal considerations:

Rhyme: that his rhymes, too, follow a scheme designed to
undermine the physical form of the poem as determined by
line. The rhymes fall internal, often insistent, but also often
hidden: obl*i*ged to leave for the *i*slands, don't *care* he said,
going down all those *stairs;* Even in the *beginning* one had
grave *misgivings;* So many mystery *guests.* And the rain that *sifts.*
These mid-line rhymes implode the phrase, fold it in two.
Strongly rhythmic, they set up patterns that run counterpoint
to those established by the line breaks, while they also cut
across meaning, which itself is often bisected by the line.
Rhyme as an inherent conflict of sound and sense, at the very
least making the word serve two separate ends. These various
violences, three modes all working at odds, result in a surface
that is constantly disrupted and must thus constantly remake
itself, which in turn calls attention to itself and discourages us
from looking for meaning elsewhere, where it isn't. Or he
poises rhymes on top of each other, both in the middle of the
line: *cloud* directly above *aloud, lay* above *clay,* and we fall
straight down through the poem as if down a mine, blindlessly
swaddled in sound, inciting a tension between gravity and its

enemies: wing and sail, my ship, now my bird, finally only reconciled in language:

my words as their feathery hulls
blow away

And there are many, many words here; in fact, it's a text in
which the common noun comes into its own—bell, river, train;
he picks inherently noble ones: lilac, garden, sun: these are
things with integrity, echoing strangely amid the ironic and last-
ing oddly longer: lamp, tower, weather—they're the short, hard
words of which the world is constructed, inviolate and categorical, never naming one alone but a timeless form that keeps on
coming down, rain, sea, song.

These words are of the same class as Cornell's objects, and the
method of composition is the same: pipe, globe, chart of the sky.
Ashbery looked up from the box and said *I am banished to an as-
teroid*. What Cornell has done with things, Ashbery has done with
words, which is to arrange them according to the schedule of the
night, the compositional principle of the constellation, the continual reconfiguration of swan, ice, owl. Of bridge, dust, hour: a
gathering of the elements that fueled 19th-century Romanticism,
all that seething nature reaching as we are reaching without ever
touching is getting taller as if the world and not the universe were
expanding, visibly abandoning something diminishing on the
shore. And this allows him to risk a Romantic treatment of beauty:

Bells chimed, the sky healed.

not the lamps purling / in the dark river

and dancers shift across the stage like leaves

Which is necessarily based on the Romantic foundation of loss,
the indelibly inaccessible: all these images are composed of immense inner distances, and again, we have recourse to cosmology,
the many references to stars, comets, moons; the universe on the
head of a pin is here sequestered,

as did Cornell in boxes,

in language: Ashbery

inserts at the precise center a gap unbridgeable because it's entirely contained, sometimes even in a single word: pier, fog, gone. An exile is not an exile except seen from the land he has left or in looking back; what we are leaving is the past, and that cannot be done. Words such as *once, anymore, were always, left behind,* and *no longer* weave in and out of the overall attempt at humor, and eventually coalesce into their own sort of home. That the exile should inhabit the unattainable: *so much*

> *that is not ours, and the tale*
> *besides, of Bedouins*

who broke out of silence as a river. It's hard to make a solid object that doesn't end. And does it echo in every box, or to have thought one face back to a light that you could breathe.

> *and the wind whispered it to the stars*
> *the people all got up to go*
> *and looked back on love*

Cy Twombly, *Hero & Leandro*
1981–84

What did you lose?
        is the sound of the sea.
                And why from a tower does
an ocean seem to stumble, to fall on its knees and bleed a pure
thin salt that could have stained a cheek had she been inclined,
but not she, who decided, after all, to go with him. That's what
grief is, an accompaniment.

Death ends the story, as it always seems to. He died at sea, as
he often does, and the sea goes on. Life handed him a lemon
and the sea made sand. Hero and Leander were like every other
pair of lovers: one died.

Hero & Leandro is an inverse ekphrasis: literature turned to a
painting. Our basic story: a woman in a tower and her lover
swimming nightly across the Hellespont guided by her lantern
who drowns of it as soon as the weather turns.

And drowns of it: water is the perfect metaphor for love—
formless, it will be shaped by outside forces, and knowing this,
becomes a wanderer upon the earth, in search of embrace, as
was Leander, as is anyone in love.

It is also the perfect metaphor for painting. Of the four elements, only land can be painted, while water, fire, and air are
among the hardest things to capture because paint is a solid object, albeit one always trying to refute that. And yet all paint is
liquid when alive, and thus all painting is the property of water,
with which it must make its peace before it can go on to anything else. Twombly addresses this by addressing the sea, over
and over, because it is that which must be crossed. *Second Voyage
to Italy, Fifty Days at Illium, Téméraire, Lepanto;* the sea is in itself a

battle, and Leander fought it, *The Wilder Shores of Love*. And there it is again, in Twombly's brush, in which a surrogate ocean of color is led shuddering across.

Life crawled out of the sea. *Hero and Leander*, 1962, numerous vigorous things emerge from an even background, and the further we travel from the center, the more specific they become until they start to take on form: a square, a tower, an X that starts to speak, to excise, one man from the sea of them. Twombly painted the first *Hero and Leander* canvas on a human scale—a great span composed of the myriad, minute conflicts and harmonies that accumulate into a human life.

From 1981 through 1984, he painted it again on an elemental scale, opening it out into Leandro, an O for ocean and a shocked exclamation in a huge sweep that breaks; the name howls in a swoop through a green and wine time across three canvases to a stark observation scrawled across a sheet of paper: oh amorous breath, he will not be breathing. When next we see him, he will have exceeded. She watched light brand the sky from her window where she'd watched all night, trying to distinguish the line between water and air. What did you lose at sea?

In the twenty years between the two projects, one language slips into another, English becomes Italian, and the story changes, which was the whole point of the oral tradition; it's a different story every voice because language is the epic that the ocean is, directionless as a painting.

By 1984, it had become a migration, this wave of unchained and uncharted emotion, of that mixture of love and despair that makes of love a mythic act and lets it participate in eternity, which love alone cannot do because it is one-sided; it requires its own opposite, which is not hate, but a despair born of the recognition of the impossibility of experiencing love's eternity. Which is why this wave is composed of opposing colors—reds heading toward purples and greens heading toward blue—opposites that nonetheless lean toward each other and crash together into two more long canvases that quell. "To paint involves a certain crisis," Twombly states.

Hero and Leander, epic poem by Christopher Marlowe, who died as he wrote it. Some say that, with Marlowe's flair for the irreverent, had he finished it, Leander might have lived.

Here where water is defined
as the where in which Aphrodite was born
                              is dissolution. (She will not
save you.) Some call it drowning, some calling
just above the pounding of the waves, some just below

the fleeting impression of a life as heaven, indebted, together
we were going to live
by my lamp, I see

that water makes us equal
everything.

We don't know how many times Leander made it across and
back in perfect safety, but we are told that it was with the arrival
of winter that all his troubles started, and we see it there in the
1962 canvas, the white foam of the colder, harder waves breaking through the surface.

Which is to imply that he died, as most of us do, of excess, of
zest (he should have been satisfied with summer), of pushing
our luck. It is precisely this tendency to exceed that constitutes
art, that is Leander in his nightly unlikely stroke after stroke.
Philip Fisher has claimed that Twombly sees an analogy to painting in Leander's nightly swimming. Swimming as an act of serial
reaching, always outward, is a suspended arriving, as is the stroke
of the brush. To show that stroke is to trust, and just beyond,
where the line turns to language, which is to say, to the absence
that each word guarantees.

And then to scrawl through that until it reaches a name. Why
is it that Twombly always seems to be writing with his wrong
hand? As if it pains him, the line that falters between language
and image. In the 1962 canvas, among the names are other
words that remain emergent, not yet fully separated, reminding
us that written language is always the line abstracted, the living
line that distilled itself from life, that stood aside and watched a
man pass.

But how easy it is to make an *A* by accident or the loop of the
lower case *L* or an *e*, and then suddenly a calle, a road through
the sea. Which, twenty years later, had shifted its balance, and all
the emergent words had consolidated into this one, this name

of all un-anchoring, of hurtling, of the one and only no Hero and no slowly redeeming symbology. Just that scream that turned to stone on touch, that remained engraved on the sky above a wave, and above which, small and illegible, something else tries to say.

Twombly is dedicated to the crisis of the line, which is the crisis of signification. Is he writing or drawing or painting these words? and what would be the difference? The written word remains symbolic; the word *ocean* for instance, remains a road sign pointing to enormous water until the word is drawn, at which point it becomes the blueprint for reality, but only when it is painted does a word actually become, a real thing in a real world, the more barely legible, the more indelible.

We picture Leander rolling over and over in the tumultuous sea, one particle that refuses homogenization, that precipitates from the saturated solution that is anything deserving of the term: *ocean:* internally overflowing: breaking out into all its own, taking place in myriad forms: arms, legs, hope.

Like the ocean, language presents the paradox of a homogeneous heterogeneity, like a Twombly painting. In an evenly chaotic medium, we find particularity, the odd particle amid a wave of light, the body borne in on the tide.

Andscape

The Serial Paintings of Etel Adnan

All its derivations—landscape, seascape, moonscape, etc.—retain a vestige of the original meaning of the suffix *scape,* which is *escape*—Chaucer 1370, "He sholde kisse his ers er that he scape"; Milton 1667, "nor did he scape," etc. They all evoke an emanation outward, a flight that left, that breath can dust, as if the self were a certain theft. The land in which it so often ends relays it onward; it is land scaping, as is its nature, farther and farther, untether, unshelter: land escaped from itself creates distance, which is what, in turn, constructs the future at that vanishing point where space turns into time. Which can only occur in two-dimensional visual art.

And so the painter reaches out to put it there, to make it fact, to future forth in parallel a world that carries on and on.

The space we see in paintings is not paint; it is space.

And so it opens up as if we could not stop and thus
we thus:

To paint a landscape is
not to depict or represent or create an illusion of
space; it is to make
which is to say

a shape that speaks

is made of various turns returned upon each other until

A landscape painting is not a painting of a given place, but the constitution of place in paint, which is why they're more accurate when abstracts. Etel Adnan has painted dozens, even hundreds, of landscapes, but even more, she has conducted a single, ongoing interrogation of landscape that cracks open in abstraction, flattens, and all endlessness is this very work always working toward.

And in so doing, she has made the act of painting into the bridge between self and world that lets consciousness disperse, lets the I overflow the body and spread out across that world as a field of bright attention traversing an earth that will not stop— and so the excess becomes manifest as a serial action, an insistence on the instance, and on its immediate repetition, on its *and,* in which it starts again, never contingent in its sovereign presence, the spark that also cracks as another world splits off. Gesture alone can enact the world as verb; "to world" they say, in which the world must show its face, and face it. Adnan's paintings all are facings, and all are facing the difficult equation that allows us to be present at the world's continual expansion.

And as is so often the case, the opposite is also true: to paint a view is also to bring that view inside, and so the painting of a field constructs an internal field, of a mountain, a mountain into, cell by cell, to occupy in soft invasion, the land beyond as internal action. If pigment

is made of various earths, is ground the rock
                                        down and rebuilds
upon a conjured surface, constructed and invested, a landscape

can never be repeated, but owns it, and thus is its own. It won. No matter where, it becomes

its particular reality singularly, which is how, within a hand that grows a mind within, a landscape is an elaboration of that internity until it shows, and so, distance differs.

And from there sifts, from mind to gesture to corporeal extension, and Adnan is the fulcrum, the fine point that invents balance through the even distribution of awareness. As with each canvas, as the earth gets larger, her fields, that enplanement of the eye, the profile of a mountain struck against sky, a reinvented world unanchored through adamant color the color of I reached a hand, and the hand went on until it too was land.

Landscape is the inevitable consequence of the fusion of hand and mind. No, landscape is the product of seeing a face from the window of a train. No, all landscapes come from a window breaking inward, but it is not a window in motion; it is, instead, one dependent upon a moment of suspension, a perfect equilibrium of improbable forces, all multiplied by color. Adnan demonstrates that color is above all shifting weight, that it sways against line, that it sharpens curves, that it swells and bends in peripheral equations that once engaged, for instance, the tree abstracted, the river beyond itself; this is their ultimate avenue of evasion, all the concrete elements of the concrete world escaping through their own essential form. In such incremental pastels, founded and added, each in its paleness, progresses, in inches, in crevasses, in a furor of precision that needs no detail. Her broad sweeps and elemental shapes founded such nuance in line and tone that all the intricate information of the natural world is present as sheer force.

Abstraction distills the argument that is or was the cataclysmic formation of the earth, which never is or was the fact but always the outward action, the act of the outside, of the verb "to outer," which is the private dimension of gesture and can only exceed. Many of Adnan's works have no frames, facilitating the scapement, a zone of evaporation, dissipation into a breakdown of sky into air and light and fraught with exuberance, its own tide coming back
and forth, a flock of air kept in mid-air

as the only limit we're likely to admit, landscape makes of that, sheer place. The infinity of space is the infinitive "to place"—a jar of water on a windowsill, and then go on. Wider than tall. As does a person, cut from the infinity that is humanity, as small a portion, and call it a self.

And so one finds oneself out walking on the side of a mountain, and paints oneself there just to stop it from further, and it furthers: person turned to world. Through recognition: one sees not a mountain, but the imperative of the corporeal, the acute tenderness of the actual, and now move on.

Etel Adnan has painted space for the past forty years, and because of that, it is almost here. There's always something we're looking for when we look out a window—it's never done abstractly; it's never done with an open mind. The open window is a specific wish, and we always find in it an emptiness. Adnan sees it and paints it full of its particularity, energy and line, mass and time, which pulls it out of itself. Her works emanate irreducible specificity—California is present here, not because it looks like it, but because it is it.

Whatever the glance falls upon, it becomes, slowly, the window of painting enables the transition—viewer into view, a quiet exchange achieved by light, which particle by particle, gets stained, which wave by wave, gets rearranged. And so a person becomes a place, by incident, by accident, who did not want but saw an opening, and then went on. Adnan's landscapes refuse the honor due to gravity; they plane above any possibility of representation, and in their refusal to touch ground, they create it.

And And

on Laurent Pariente's *White Walls,* Musée Bourdelle,
Paris, 2006, which can be seen on a number of sites by
searching under Laurent Pariente's name

The relation of white to wall: are lightly blinded, we walk up to
it, almost invisible in the way that a mirror can render unrecog-
nizable—we walk *up to* echo *into*—"When you touch a wall, the
wall touches back" (Pariente).

The walls in Laurent Pariente's work are accretions of inter-
secting shadows, making us realize that a shadow is the principle
upon which all that is impenetrable operates—by situating the
shadow on the inside. And the white evaporates. Which is a rising up, and the wall aloft, and the uncanny resistance of chalk.

The intricate interlacing of walls that composed his *White
Walls* exhibition at the Musée Bourdelle was in fact achieved by
a single wall splitting off from and turning back on itself, a single line wandering at right angles until it filled the entire room.

With room after room. It is through the white that the wall-
as-limit becomes wall-as-unfolding, which is wall-as-wanderer—a
series of articulations until it achieves the dimension of a mansion—uncountable rooms and no doors between, and every
now and then, a corner slit open, a rift from floor to ceiling seeing into other rooms and on to the other therefrom: doorway
without door after door

without an end to the soon

and through the doorway he saw

and the wall opened for him

throughout a white afternoon

and in one small room you'll find
a man bending down to pick up something small,
a piece of paper, folding over, a white after white we have tried
to repeat
but a lengthened difference
was my home as in shadow;
I lived in a series of interlocking rooms that can carry.

And the shadow carried him home.

When a doorway outnumbers its door, we have an uncountable opening in the shape of the empty, and in glancing to the
left, in a series of flight, the angled guest.
Thus a doorway is always a distance, and if there's a face in it,
our corridors have corridors within them

and he traveled seven days without ever leaving the house.
Laurent Pariente's walls are broken and something white follows you from ocean to ocean.
Laurent Pariente enters the house alone; the body becomes
its own room, and so he must walk on, which is an accumulative
art, an intersection of time and space that is the body slightly
lost, which is the future until he had no house.
If once a white shadow, over, wing, over
want under
want either
and washed it asunder
these were the corridors we wandered to pieces
gone acre, now naked, what army of silent
To walk into the deaf house, the chalk house, the flayed
house that Pariente has built a house in which there are no
rooms; there are only corridors leading to *walk* into the thought
house, the sparrow home, the mathematical hand. We are con-
strained to live in houses, where starts anemia, thus amnesia,
and are dreaming: the houses of the mind fall for miles. And it's
relaxing, a matter of slowly giving, and often the fall is lateral,
and you walk on without thinking.
Laurent Pariente has set out to use silence as a building material, and from there devolve houses composed entirely of angles.

If sighted down to the vanishing point, if the earth goes ajar. And she leaned on the doorframe as if she had ages. Which makes the days harder.

Which is to say, geometry and light constitute a forest, which is in turn defined by its aleatory, its arbitrary, its errance is the geometry of a threshold seen across a salt plain delivered at regular intervals he placed a statue that became a monument because an echo becomes visible the more the forest grows larger from your listening, from your leaning in as though you were listening even harder
are the days.

Space occurs in pieces.

Pariente sculpts only what cannot be touched.

Interviewer: What do you think touch is?
Pariente: White.
Interviewer: What do you think white is?
Pariente: The face on its way.
Interviewer: What do you think a wall is?
Pariente: Something, anything, that opens itself because it hears a slight sound and so turns around a little too quickly and cracks open at the spine, simply flays its own vertebral column, atmosphere layered, which is to say air—there it turned; a wall is a spiral stair in a slower mirror, which is a wall ironed out by fire and I'm caught on the top step.

Wandering such hallways in the light
disturbs the careful balance of inside and out.
Interviewer: What do you think inside is?
Pariente: I thought of adding a small red square.

Quand le corps est une phrase à venir

Claude Royet-Journoud

Grammar   on the horizontal
one of the bases of common

to say it is moving, and then, as in the old song, "Let me count
the ways."

                              in the public gardens, which is where,
naturally, he

These issues are raised again in each book—a body surfaces
more thoroughly, a more thorough surface that moves toward
continually; the page becomes fluid, refusing determined direction and offering space

in which living could take place, a space that responds to the
motion of visual as well as verbal language. You say   (for instance)   fragile   (and it
                        cracks outward in those shapes that incite
associates. You
                        said

                              fragility

            two or three simultaneous readings   and not only

refusing stasis   *seen*
                        Though he can say, *"It is also a work of suppression.*
Which is not to say that there is under the text another text lacking."

"and the world becomes legible"

"finally what interests me is this mystery of the literal."

a glance, spliced
between two opposing and moving windows
and there he is doing kind things, single, small,
so kind they're uncommon. Literal smile
tangible seal.

"what I think about accident"

And the "mystery of the literal" leads
inexorably to a poetics of banality, to a progressive stripping away
of artifice, giving him an unremitting contact with the surface.
Tangible text. Such contact includes the paradox that though
the surface is completely visible, it is never completely seen because it is never completed.

Text that battles entropy, that tendency for energy as well as
difference within a closed system to dissipate. His work battles it
simply by remaining open, by a moment's dislocation within the
system, a misplaced distance, a voice from the street filtered
through glass.

"I think about accident"

In place of narrative or imagistic continuity, a particular type of
motion animates the surface of his page, making the page into
a body, which in turn incorporates first the body of the writer
and then that of the reader into its world.

mains innombrables

(If sound were salt)

en avance sur sa propre main, il tourne le dos
(No argument this fine, this sieved, nor would proof)

la main prise dans la page

(All remains is)

la main passe

A man in a park blends in with the trees. I watch him at a slight distance while he does not know that anyone is watching him there is nothing there to watch a man thus caught in the world of the trees there seem to be various men who refuse the distinction of the seam between the body and the world and the body and the trees and the world becomes legible.

main intarrissable

He's waiting for someone to come back with coffee, two shots, each one in its tiny white plastic cup with its tiny white plastic oar submerged and emerging, watching the children playing and now the playing and the sitting and the watching and they're growing and you can't see them in the photograph though there seems to be a disturbance or perhaps a stirring would be a better word there in the air.

Comme si dans la pierre circulait une main
vive. Tous les gestes qu'on oublie

In another description of his working process, he has used the example of ichnology, the science of traces, which is used to re-create the bodies of long-extinct animals from a few shards of bone or from fossilized footprints. Similarly, in his work, the reader is in the presence of evidence, which always operates as positive indication of an absence. The ichnologist's project is that of a detective.

And is particularly drawn to the American "hard-boiled" variety, in which the detective operates single-handedly between the separately authoritative realms of the police and criminal worlds, often arriving at a solution that avoids submission to either.

(When seen from a distance, the person is a shape with its own idiosyncratic grace and never static but might shift as you stand at the edge of the line of trees with the two steaming cups

in your hand and watch the way one shape balances against another, the others, the ones that move.)

appuyée contre les deux images

in between
ce visage qui brusquement s'ouvre

the trees there is

in a green metal chair living on green

like the leaves of some trees (the ginkgo) used to heal.

UNDER DISCUSSION
Annie Finch and Marilyn Hacker, General Editors
Donald Hall, Founding Editor

Volumes in the Under Discussion series collect reviews and essays about individual poets. The series is concerned with contemporary American and English poets about whom the consensus has not yet been formed and the final vote has not been taken. Titles in the series include:

On Frank Bidart: Fastening the Voice to the Page
  edited by Liam Rector and Tree Swenson
On Louise Glück: Change What You See
  edited by Joanne Feit Diehl
On James Tate
  edited by Brian Henry
Robert Hayden
  edited by Laurence Goldstein and Robert Chrisman
Charles Simic
  edited by Bruce Weigl
On Gwendolyn Brooks
  edited by Stephen Caldwell Wright
On William Stafford
  edited by Tom Andrews
Denise Levertov
  edited with an introduction by Albert Gelpi
The Poetry of W. D. Snodgrass
  edited by Stephen Haven
On the Poetry of Philip Levine
  edited by Christopher Buckley
James Wright
  edited by Peter Stitt and Frank Graziano
Anne Sexton
  edited by Steven E. Colburn
On the Poetry of Galway Kinnell
  edited by Howard Nelson
Robert Creeley's Life and Work
  edited by John Wilson
On the Poetry of Allen Ginsberg
  edited by Lewis Hyde
Reading Adrienne Rich
  edited by Jane Roberta Cooper
Elizabeth Bishop and Her Art
  edited by Lloyd Schwartz and Sybil P. Estess

Printed and bound by CPI Group (UK) Ltd, Croydon, CR0 4YY

13/04/2025

14656532-0001